from india

from india

food, family & tradition

kumar & suba mahadevan

MURDOCH BOOKS

This book is dedicated to my family, who are the strength and pillars of my life: my 'Patti' grandmother, who lay the foundation for my culinary journey, my amma for pampering my palate, and my appa for all his guidance and support. My 'better half', the beautiful Suba, for encouraging me, being a part of my life and having patience. Your tireless efforts in researching for this book, travelling with me to corners of India, and for braving all the meat and seafood prep despite being a strict vegetarian. And our sons: Abhinav and Akilesh, for sweetening our lives and for assisting us at Abhi's and Aki's.

contents

foreword

In 1994, Australia was well on the way to becoming one of the great food nations. Restaurateurs including Gilbert Lau and Stephanie Alexander in Melbourne and Janni Kyritsis, Tony Bilson, Neil Perry and Tetsuya Wakuda in Sydney were leading the charge.

I was the food critic for the *Sydney Morning Herald*, sharing the role with Helen Greenwood. The Mod Oz–French style was well established, and I made it my mission to search Sydney for great ethnic restaurants. Gilbert Lau's Flower Drum had shown us how good Cantonese cuisine can be, with stunningly good Australian produce combined with authentic Chinese techniques; Tetsuya was inventing his own modern Japanese/French hybrid cuisine to worldwide acclaim, but the other great ethnic cuisine, Indian, was a mess. I encountered fire-engine-red kebabs, cardboard-dry tandoori chicken, searingly hot vindaloos, soggy breads, and curries with boring, singular tastes. Under all the bad spicing lurked indifferent ingredients. This was an insult to a great cuisine. In London, Bombay Brasserie and The Red Fort had proven Indian cuisine had a place at the very top, so what was wrong with Australia, where Indian equalled takeaway or something cheap and nasty?

I stumbled into Abhi's for a quick lunch on my way from a business meeting. It looked like any other suburban Indian, and my expectations were not high. It was a true revelation. The kebabs were not red, the tandoori chicken oozed with juices and flavour, tandoori lamb chops were clearly superior produce, the curries had an incredible array of complex, fresh tastes and the breads were perfect. This was great traditional Indian food, cooked with proper technique and passion. I was back the next night, which ended with Kumar proudly showing me his spice-grinding machine with which he made his own masalas every day.

I soon published a review, with the headline 'The Search is Over'. Sydney finally had a great Indian restaurant. People flocked to Abhi's. Many restaurants have such a crush of diners after a favourable review and then sink into obscurity, but Kumar welcomed the new diners, became their friends, introduced them to the complexities of Indian food and went on to open Aki's.

Kumar at first wanted to take traditional Indian food more upmarket at Aki's, but I suggested he do something different. Show us the new Indian cuisine, show us the regional specialities, give us dishes we've never heard of I urged. Kumar promised to serve the same food that was eaten at the best tables in Mumbai. Having been to India with Kumar I reckon he has done better. Kumar has simply invented his own style of Indian cuisine, based on classic Indian technique but with a wonderful Aussie accent thanks to our great produce and Kumar's unending passion to be the best.

Kumar and Suba are totally dedicated to their restaurants, and I'm sure we will continue to be surprised. For them, the search is not over.

Les Luxford

vannakkam
welcome to our table

Vannakkam is a Tamil saying meaning 'welcome'. The people of this state, where I was born, have a belief that serving food to others is a service to mankind. Share our culture, family, traditions and our journey around India in this book, and learn to cook the food we love most.

kumar

Our family has an astrologer we turn to for advice when we need to make important decisions. Astrology is an ancient science and we are fortunate to have a good astrologer. He helped me find my wife, Suba, and we've been married for twenty-five years. It seemed like an odd match, but he was right. My life hasn't turned out the way some expected, but I couldn't be happier. Perhaps some things are written in the stars, but we can't always see it.

I grew up in a town called Tirunelveli, in the state of Tamil Nadu, near the southern tip of India. It sits on the western side of the Thamirabarani River, 700 kilometres southwest of the capital, Chennai. Everyone knew our place as House Number 108. I lived there with my grandmother Meenakshi, her two sons, my dad and uncle, and their wives, my mum and aunty, and my brother, who now lives in Australia, a sister and four cousins.

Patti, a term of respect for grandmother, is the biggest influence on my cooking. My grandmother is the SALT, the prime ingredient that shaped my childhood. Patti had an amazing sense of smell, which is something I got from her. Smell is my greatest sense. It's my driving force in the kitchen and a key part of taste. My chefs tell me I should have been a sniffer dog. Patti Meenakshi never cooked once her children married. She sat in the corner of the kitchen watching her daughters-in-law, telling them what to do, especially the order in which spices should be added, and then sniffing the air saying, 'That's burnt!' or 'The aroma is lost!' She was a perfectionist.

When I started doing that to my mum, Gomathi, she responded, 'You're worse than my mother-in-law!'

We are vegetarians and Patti was very firm and strict about what made a good meal. It had to include four different vegetables, two types of lentils, two chutneys, pappadoms and pickles, and two rice dishes or chapatis, but all in small amounts. She preferred variety and quality to quantity. To this day, I like my meals the same way, with all the condiments, even when I get home from work at midnight and feel hungry. My wife thinks I'm a little crazy, but she understands why.

Patti would serve us when we came home from school for lunch and teach us about the right flavour combinations and how to balance a meal. She had mystery tasting and testing games, asking us if we could pick up hidden spices and ingredients. Meals were often shared with friends and neighbours and with Patti in charge it made them fun, loving and also educational.

My grandmother is the SALT, the prime
ingredient that shaped my childhood.

By the time I was seven, I was very curious about flavour and taste, but Mum and Dad would say to me, 'Control your tongue!' They meant you won't be academic if you give importance to your tongue. Your brain will go numb from eating so much and you won't concentrate on study. That's a Brahmin philosophy. I was raised Hindu as a Brahmin, the priestly class. Brahmins are quite academic and intellectual. They're not necessarily gourmets. They like clean tastes. I've changed a lot since then, but my food is still about clean, clear flavours.

Everyone expected me to become a doctor or engineer, but I'd sneak into the kitchen while pretending to study. I was eight when Patti taught me how to make rasam, a lentil soup that's a staple in every Southern Indian meal. Many people think it's simple, but there's a lot of complexity and subtlety in that simplicity. Patti emphasised the Ayurvedic nature of food. The term comes from two Sanskrit words meaning longevity and knowledge. It's a form of alternative medicine and there are six kinds of rasam, made according to the seasons and family needs. There are different rasams for varying ailments, from pepper rasam for colds and flu to lime or tamarind rasam for a healthy heart.

Patti would say, 'Food is the essence of existence'. Our family keeps her recipes and habit of healthy criticism alive to this day.

I was sixteen and had just started an economics degree at Madras University when my family's fortunes fell. Dad made and sold steel utensils, but the business collapsed and owed huge debts. I lasted less than a month at uni. My father couldn't support the family and we were under a lot of financial pressure when a distant friend suggested the Madras Catering College to me. I was passionate about wanting to cook and jumped at the chance, but I struggled to convince my parents it was the right decision. I wanted to help repay the money Dad owed. A full scholarship for the three-year course helped, but it caused a lot of family tension, because it wasn't seen as the right career for a Brahmin. It was a time of upheaval and BITTER struggles to go against my upbringing. One relative refused to eat at the same table with me for several months. Chefs were below him and by definition, unintelligent. I was devastated, but was about to become even more of a rebel.

My training began with a big shock on my very first day. Eating meat is a sin for Brahmins, who are even wary of onions and garlic, which are considered aphrodisiacs. I puked when I had my first mouthful of meat. I ran out of the classroom and kept vomiting. I couldn't understand the flavour or texture. I tried to avoid it, but really I had no choice if I wanted to be a good cook. It took about four months before I was comfortable with it. I trained my palate and got used to the flavours by tasting sauces rather than the meat itself.

At the end of my first year, I got a summer job at the five-star Taj Mahal Palace Hotel in Bombay (now Mumbai). I was seventeen and the least experienced of all the interns, but had unlimited energy. Conscious of the money my family owed, I signed up for double and sometimes triple shifts, working eighteen consecutive days and staying with an aunt who lived 90 minutes' train ride away. As luck would have it, they put me in the butchery section under a grumpy old chef. My first job was taking the skin off chicken drumsticks. By day two I was boning them out. The cuts and bandaids on my fingers reminded me to focus on getting better. I learned on the job, handling cuts of meats I'd never seen before and becoming an expert. I worked in every section under Cyrus Todiwala, a Parsi chef who now runs London's Café Spice Namasté. Between shifts, I'd work in room service to get more experience. But I had one big problem. I spoke Tamil, not Hindi, the language of Bombay. The others teased me and made up fake terms for the kitchen techniques I was learning, but I picked up enough to get by.

My fear of meat vanished and by the time I was back at college, I was bartering with my classmates to trim their meat in return for prep I didn't enjoy, like chopping onions. I graduated in 1979, aged nineteen and was offered jobs in nearly every five-star hotel in India. I went back to the Taj on a salary of 640 rupees, about $80 a month and was fast-tracked, graduating in half the time. By then I also understood French and Chinese flavours, as well as loving Bombay's street food, which we'd go out to eat in our time off. This was the boost I needed — the SOUR slap to wake up my spirit and sharpen my mind.

I'd send half my wage home to my family, but it still wasn't enough to pay my dad's debts, even when my pay doubled. My mum needed an operation and once again fate intervened. The Sheraton opened a new hotel in Basrah, Iraq, in 1981 and I went to work there. My salary jumped tenfold. The only downside was I was moving to a war zone. The Iran–Iraq war was entering its second year and we were 20 kilometres from the enemy border. We had front-row seats for the conflict's regular shelling.

Home was caravan-style accommodation in the nearby staff village, but we had no life beyond the hotel — a colleague who ventured out for cigarettes came home with shrapnel in his leg — and its 40 centimetre thick walls meant it doubled as a bomb shelter. When the bombardments intensified, we'd move into the hotel, sometimes for days, sometimes for weeks. The longest lockdown period was nearly two months. By 1984 the situation had deteriorated further and many senior executives had left. Produce was scarce. We'd go for months without eggs or butter. My father's debts were now repaid and I'd had enough and returned to Bombay.

My next adventure came in the form of a newspaper article in the *Times of India*. The Tea Board of India and Air India had joined forces to open two restaurants in London and Sydney to promote our nation and wanted chefs. London sounded ideal. I got the job, but they sent me to Australia in August 1985. I arrived in Sydney with two other chefs, on a one-way ticket, with a permanent resident's visa. The only things I knew about my new home were that the cricket was great and that women sunbathed topless. The first thing I noticed was clear blue sky and vivid colours, but within six hours of arriving, we started our first shift at Mayur, in Sydney's Martin Place. It was a three-level fine diner serving traditional Indian food and seated 100 people. It attracted celebrities including Elton John, Mick Jagger and the King of Bahrain. Everyone loved watching us work the open tandoor, but the kitchen was much smaller than the hotels I was used to. Conditions were tough. We worked 96-hour weeks over six days for poor pay and had signed four-year contracts with a clause that said if we left, our parents had to pay a large penalty. We shared a single-bedroom city apartment with three mattresses on the floor. I knew nothing but hard work and my goal at the time was to survive.

A year on, I wanted to settle down, so I told my father I wanted to find a traditional Indian girl to marry. Despite all my adventures, I'm proud of my culture, which is very valuable to me and very easy to lose. I'm keen to preserve it and pass it down to my children. My father put an ad in the paper asking for an 'alliance'. It's such a funny word, but looking back on my marriage to Suba, it now seems just right.

this was the boost i needed — the SOUR slap
to wake up my spirit and sharpen my mind.

I knew nothing about her, but our astrologer told my parents we were a good match. We seemed like opposites — I'm loud, energetic and full of ambition, while Suba's shy, quiet and calm — but the astrologer looked for compatibility in the long term and like the spices used in Indian cooking, the strength of one is mitigated and enhanced by the subtlety of the other.

Suba sent me a studio photo, but she looked too serious. The first thing that attracts me in a woman is her eyes. They speak a lot of things, but I couldn't tell from this photo, so I asked for another one and she sent one of her with her young cousin. I could see her playfulness and smile. We exchanged letters, which took two weeks to arrive, and phone calls, but didn't meet until ten days before our wedding. I couldn't afford the time or money to fly to India for our engagement. Just three months passed between the 'alliance' being formed and our marriage. The engagement photos arrived just as I was leaving for India. Our traditional wedding in Chennai, in July 1987, took two days, with thousands of people attending. It went on a bit too long for my liking, before our three-day honeymoon in a hill resort called Kodaikanal. Finally Suba and I had a chance to talk.

I came back to Australia for work and my wife followed three months later with my mother. The astrologer sent my mother, saying she had to stay until Suba and I understood each other. She was the bridge. He told her, 'You've got to control your son and be supportive to your daughter-in-law and shield her from this devil,' which is me. I call a spade a spade and I'm pretty blunt, whereas Suba's the opposite.

My father-in-law said, 'My daughter's a great cook,' but after we were married, I discovered she didn't know how to cook. I asked him, 'Why did you stick up for your daughter?' Of course Suba's a great cook now, although she's still vegetarian.

Mum stayed for twelve months until our first son was born. I used to meet Suba in the park for a date between shifts, just to see her alone. Work was tough. A friend was making three times my wage elsewhere, so I knew I was underpaid. I was forced to go back into the kitchen just a few hours after our son, Abhinav (Abhi) was born in 1988. I carried that hurt for many years, but it taught me an important lesson in how NOT to treat people.

I was desperately unhappy and wanted to leave so I told my dad, who consulted the astrologer. He said I had a brighter future ahead, but now is not the time to leave, so I stuck on. As it happened, Mayur failed after two years and suddenly I was free. I was sick of Indian food and wanted to cook anything but curries. Suba was a tower of strength. She said I should not give up my talent.

I was cooking at Sorrentino café in Sydney's Circular Quay in late 1989 and became friends with the owner, Doug Moxon. We decided to open an Indian restaurant together. It took six months, but we found a place in North Strathfield and in 1990, Abhi's, named after my son, opened. Doug was a partner in the business for seven years and remains a good friend.

I wanted Abhi's to be different. There were no samosas or pakoras on the menu. I wanted both authentic and contemporary flavours to showcase the regional beauty of Indian cuisine. Palak patta chaat, a street-food classic, using chickpea batter–coated spinach leaves with three chutneys and cumin-infused yoghurt, was on the first menu and soon became a signature dish. Dosa, the lentil and rice pancakes from my southern birthplace, eaten with the hand, became an instant hit.

Our second son, Akilesh, was born in 1991 and during those years we struggled until Les Luxford reviewed us in the *Sydney Morning Herald* in April 1994. He said he'd found the best Indian food in Sydney. Suddenly, we were an 'overnight success' and there were queues down the street. It was all hands on deck and I called Suba in to help in the restaurant in the evenings.

I realised Suba's true strength when a trusted staff member robbed us of a large amount of money. We were young, married four years, with two small children and fighting to make ends meet. I was shattered, absolutely devastated and I cried. Suba said something I'll remember for the rest of my life, 'This person has robbed you only of money, let him not rob you of your mental strength'.

After that, I woke up and it really built my confidence. Suba's so sharp and strong. She's behind all my success: the driving force and strength in all the decisions we make. Now she corrects me all the time and she's my biggest critic. She wrote the twenty-first anniversary menu for Abhi's. That's how well she understands what we do. I am so proud of her. Suba is my spice girl and a must SPICE in all my endeavours.

We opened Aki's on the newly restored Woolloomooloo finger wharf, the first in a row of hip waterside eateries, in November 2003. It was a very brave thing to do because Indian food is still not accepted at the fine-dining level in Australia. There's a lot of perceptions we need to correct about Indian food and that's what I'm trying to do there. We focus on seafood. The signature dish, crab iddiappam is a fine example of this fusion of tradition, innovation and great local produce. It seems to be working. In 2011, Aki's was awarded a chef's hat in the *Sydney Morning Herald Good Food Guide*.

My other passions are photography, wine and travel. I love Australian wine and I'm very proud of the wine lists at both restaurants. I've also been researching the history and regionality of Indian cooking and every year, we visit our homeland to discover and better understand the flavours of India. It's amazing how the same dish can change so dramatically in appearance, aroma, taste and texture in just a few kilometres.

My boys are now in their twenties and help out in the restaurants too. To have such a happy worklife and family is the SWEET balance I've been looking for. We are a very close family and we still have quite a strong relationship with our astrologer. He's close to 80 now and still tells me do this, don't do that ... He's even advised us when our children should be married. We trust him completely. After all, he was right about Suba and me.

to have such a happy worklife and family is the **SWEET** balance I've been looking for.

suba

Kumar has kaivasnai, a Tamil word that means 'hands that give flavour'. I don't come from a big foodie family. We just ate what was given to us, which was very simple. My father's only comment about food was if a dish needed less or more salt. It took me a while to understand that what Kumar says isn't meant to hurt — and he offers criticism freely and frequently. Now I tell him, can you please tell me the truth? I don't want him to say something just to be nice. Even my mother asked Kumar for help to improve her cooking.

My father, Krishnamurthi, was an engineer for All India Radio and every few years, he'd be transferred, so I lived in lots of different regions. I was born in Chennai, started school in Jodhpur and finished it in Sangli. After a few years in Mumbai, I moved back to Chennai, graduated with a commerce degree and took a job as an announcer at Chennai Railway Station. My father's travels meant that I spoke four state languages — Hindi, Marwadi, Tamil, Marathi — as well as English. Kumar only spoke Tamil.

I found out about my marriage accidentally, overhearing a conversation. I discovered that our horoscopes were already matched and Kumar's parents were coming to see me. Suddenly my life was taking a very different turn. Girls of my caste married doctors and lawyers, not chefs. I was twenty-one, so shy and confused too, so I simply left everything to my parents. There was no compulsion from our parents that we had to get married. At any time we could say no, but I still felt the pressure. Our destiny was overpowering our emotions.

I was worried about how to settle in Australia, especially since I'd never left India; however, my age was an advantage and I believed I could adapt. When they sent me Kumar's photo, I wondered how tall he would be. He had sunnies on, so I wanted another photo. I did think he had a nice smile. I didn't have any photographs of myself, so I went to a studio to have one taken and sent it to him, but he thought it looked too serious and wanted another one.

The next step was a phone call, but I'd never made an international one before. His parents had a phone

at their house, so I'd go over there to talk to him. I was so nervous. Kumar is very talkative and straight away he started asking questions. I didn't know whether to speak in English or in Tamil and I don't think I answered any of the first few questions. He asked me if I knew how to cook. I said yes. I thought he meant the basic, simple cooking I grew up with. I simply kept saying yes to anything. It was a nervous yes. There was a lot of pressure on me. I thought if I said yes, everything would be alright. The only confidence I had was that if I said yes, I'd be able to do it. But I also felt very stressed after that first call and wondered what the next one would be about.

My initial impression was Kumar was full of life and seemed so worldly. On the second call, he made a lot of suggestions, such as driving and photography courses. After a while we both began to look forward to our calls, then Kumar asked his younger brother to go see me. He turned out to be an absolute contrast to Kumar and told his elder brother, 'She's too good for you, you got more than you asked for'.

We had the traditional first meeting at my parents' place, just ten days before our marriage. Kumar's parents had warned me that he's very fast, very loud and very aggressive. My heart was pounding and my hands were shaking as I tried to pour coffees. Everyone was watching and I was the centre of attention. I was so shy I didn't even look up to his face. After ten minutes Kumar said, 'I want to have a word with her separately.' He asked if I'd done the things he asked me to do and once again I just

working with kumar has brought us even
closer together. we have a common goal
in the success of our restaurants.

kept saying yes, yes. I didn't want to do anything to break things up and I was afraid.

One thing I really like about Kumar is there's an old-fashioned side to him. We share a faith in our parents and astrologer. My comfort was that the astrologer said our marriage would work. Yet here I was marrying a chef and I didn't even know how to use a knife and fork! After the wedding, he took me to a five-star hotel for a meal, but I'd only ever eaten with my hands or a spoon.

I was shocked when I discovered he ate meat. It never occurred to me, but it's inevitable if you're a chef. I started to accept it and because he thoroughly understands and respects the background we come from, he's fine with the fact that I remain vegetarian to this day.

Compromise and understanding are keys to a successful married life. Opposite poles attract — this really made sense to us.

Our honeymoon in Kodaikanal was the first time we were alone and that's when our life together really started. The first thing he said was, 'You know, I talk a lot.' I thought what am I going to answer to this? It's true, so I said, 'I know, I listen a lot,' and Kumar replied, 'That's good enough!'

He's too adventurous and we went rowing in a small canoe on the river. I knew nothing about water or even swimming and suddenly I got tired and wanted to give up. Kumar said, 'No, this is how life is going to be. We've got to get across, so you'd better row,' and we did it together. That moment summed up how our life together would be.

I realised right from the day I got married that the drive for perfection was a key part of Kumar. He wants everything right and if he wants something done, he'll get it done now, whereas I'm slow and steady.

When I came to Australia, I was shocked and wondered how I'd manage this person — his loud voice against my soft shy nature, his fast movements against my slow reactions, his short temper against my cool nature; so I kept quiet and followed him. Adjusting was difficult initially but then love started kicking in and we felt very comfortable with each other. Two months after arriving in Sydney, I had a job working in administration with the New South Wales Police. I stayed there for fifteen years and it gave me a chance to explore the city, its people and culture and broaden my views on life.

When the restaurant review came out in 1994 Kumar said the restaurant was really busy and he wanted me to come and help him. I had no experience, but he didn't listen. He threw me in the deep end as usual and the first thing I did was carry prawns to a table. There's a picture of God in the restaurant and at the end of service I went and prayed, asking, 'What am I doing?' But then people were happy and smiling, so why would I think it was a sin? At the end of the day, I told Kumar I really enjoyed it. He brought my strength and confidence out of me. I didn't know how to do it. Kumar did. Working with Kumar has brought us even closer together. We have a common goal in the success of our restaurants.

We travel to India on a regular basis for inspiration. Kumar loves rediscovering bygone recipes from master cooks and visiting housewives who stick to the old traditional style of cooking. He then weaves it into the food at Abhi's and Aki's.

Kumar asked me to design the twenty-first anniversary menu for Abhi's. Can you imagine it, when I'm still a vegetarian? It was such a success. This is how he brings out my strengths. I have become an integral part of his life, his business and everything around him. Kumar and I are now so dependent on each other, and our children have seen the success of our lives and how we balance each other. We have a wonderful, close family and we are so proud of our children. It's amazing to see what we've achieved from an arranged marriage. Even today, when we go to see our astrologer he recalls how we met and says, 'See, I told you.'

salt

SALT IS A PRIME INGREDIENT IN SHAPING LIVES.
Without salt there is no flavour. It is the mother of all ingredients: that's the first lesson Patti, my grandmother Meenakshi, taught me. She only had to smell a curry to tell if it was seasoned properly and, thankfully, that skill passed on to me. Understanding its importance is the key to good food. My hand still shakes when I add salt. It's the one and only sensitive ingredient that makes or breaks a meal. My grandma was the salt of my childhood. She was a walking, talking recipe book with strict commands to be followed. She has always been the inspiration for my cooking, and she fed my hunger for knowledge well.

To get the best result, add salt during cooking, rather than sprinkling it on food at a later stage, but always be careful because if you add too much, the excess cannot be removed.

Natural salt is considered the prime spice in Ayurvedic cooking, as it stimulates digestion and of course is an essential part of life. There's a special volcanic salt from India called kala namak or sanchal that is believed to have medicinal qualities. It is also known as black salt, but when ground it's more pinky-grey in colour. Kala namak has a slight bitterness and, most distinctively, a pungent sulfurous (rotten egg) smell, and it is an essential part of chaat masala (a spice mix used in chaat).

Always use good-quality salt flakes for cooking, even though they are a little more expensive, instead of table salt, which has a number of additives, including anti-caking agents. Maldon sea salt from England and Australian Murray River pink salt are two of my favourites for cooking.

When you're choosing what salt to use, put a little on the tip of your tongue and taste its strength. This sounds contradictory, but you don't want it to be too salty. A good salt has quite complex flavours and even a slight sweetness.

Sea salt acts as a balance between sweetness and acidity, and reduces sourness and increases sweetness, which is why it's also important in desserts.

A curry without salt is considered inauspicious in Hindu culture. Its importance is such that after someone dies, a feast is prepared after ten days without using salt to cook, so that the soul leaves its earthly desires and finds peace.

All these things I learned at the elbow of my grandma. I hope to keep her memory alive and pass on her wisdom in the following recipes, which are an extension of our family meals.

grandma's dal

braised lentils

My grandma Meenakshi would always insist that this dal be cooked every other day. The 'moong' was her favourite dal, being easy to digest. She preferred her dal with a bit of extra asafoetida. Meenakshi was very particular about her diet and she never even allowed onion or garlic to enter her kitchen.

100 g (3½ oz) moong dal (green gram) (see glossary)

100 g (3½ oz) toor dal (yellow lentils) (see glossary)

1 teaspoon ground turmeric

6 small green chillies, halved lengthways

80 g (2¾ oz/⅓ cup) ghee (see glossary)

1 teaspoon cumin seeds

1 tablespoon finely grated ginger

2 tomatoes, sliced

½ teaspoon asafoetida (see glossary)

roughly chopped coriander (cilantro), to garnish

Wash and rinse the moong dal and toor dal and put in a large saucepan. Add sufficient water to cover the dal by about 1 cm (½ inch). Add the turmeric and chilli and bring to the boil, then simmer, uncovered for 35 minutes or until the dal has completely broken down, adding a little more water if it is looking dry.

Meanwhile, heat the ghee in a frying pan over medium heat. Once the ghee is hot, add the cumin seeds and cook for 30 seconds. Add the ginger and cook for 2 minutes. Add the tomato and asafoetida and cook for 1 minute.

Add to the dal and cook for a further 5 minutes. Season with salt and serve garnished with coriander.

avial

vegetables in yoghurt curry

This is one of the very early recipes my mum taught me. It is a very simple and easy mix of vegetables with a very clean taste. The secret is to cook all of the vegetables at different stages to preserve their crunchiness. This is predominantly cooked with root vegetables. In Kerala they add peeled jackfruit seeds. If the timing is not right, it can end up as a vegetable mash.

70 g (2½ oz/½ cup) grated coconut (see glossary)

3 small green chillies, roughly chopped

½ teaspoon cumin seeds

95 g (3¼ oz/⅓ cup) plain thick yoghurt, beaten

1 potato, cut into finger-sized batons

1 sweet potato (about 400 g/14 oz), cut into finger-sized batons

1 carrot, cut into finger-sized batons

3 drumsticks (see glossary), cut into 5 cm (2 inch) pieces

½ taro or white sweet potato (yam) (about 200 g/7 oz), cut into finger-sized batons

1 green banana, cut into finger-sized batons

1 small eggplant (aubergine), cut into finger-sized batons

10 green beans, halved

2 tablespoons vegetable or sunflower oil

10 curry leaves

1 tablespoon coconut oil (see glossary) (see tip)

Put the grated coconut, green chilli and cumin seeds in a small spice grinder with 2 tablespoons of water and grind to a smooth paste. This step is very important as it provides the texture of the finished dish. Transfer to a bowl and stir the beaten yoghurt into this paste.

The vegetables need to be cooked until they are just tender and soft to the bite, but not mushy, and in just enough water to cover them. Put the potato, sweet potato, carrot and drumstick into a heavy-based saucepan over medium–high heat and pour over enough boiling water to just cover the vegetables. Season with salt.

After 2 minutes, add the taro, banana and eggplant, cook for 6 minutes, then add the beans and cook for 2 minutes.

When the vegetables are almost done, add the coconut paste and cook over low heat for 5–7 minutes — the yoghurt tends to split, hence the need for the heat to be low, and the coconut acts as a binding agent to prevent the yoghurt curdling.

While the vegetables are cooking, heat the vegetable oil in a small saucepan over high heat, add the curry leaves and fry for about 20 seconds. Drain on paper towel.

To finish the dish, pour over the cold coconut oil and scatter over the fried curry leaves.

Tip: If cold coconut oil is too pungent for your taste, heat the oil before pouring it over the dish.

kaali dal

black lentils

This dish is found all over India. In the north, it is called 'maa ki dal' and is made with the starchy and wholesome urad dal (black lentils) but in the south it is made with toor dal (yellow lentils), which have a very low starch content. This is due to the different climates; North India gets much colder so the food reflects the need for a heavier and richer diet, and spices such as cloves, cardamom, cinnamon, ginger, black pepper and nutmeg are used in cooking to keep the body warm, whereas in the hotter south, spices such as chilli and garlic are consumed in high amounts to help the body sweat and keep it cool.

300 g (10½ oz/1⅓ cups) urad dal (black lentils) (see glossary), soaked overnight in 2 litres (70 fl oz) water

100 g (3½ oz/½ cup) dried red kidney beans, soaked overnight (see tip)

250 g (9 oz) tomatoes, roughly chopped, or 170 g (6 oz) tomato paste (concentrated purée)

100 g (3½ oz) butter, chopped

1 tablespoon finely grated ginger

1 tablespoon crushed garlic

1 tablespoon vegetable or sunflower oil

1 teaspoon cumin seeds

1 red onion, thinly sliced

1 teaspoon red chilli powder

halved cherry tomatoes, thin (pouring) cream, finely shredded ginger, finely chopped coriander (cilantro) and softened butter (optional), to garnish

SERVES 4 AS PART OF A SHARED MEAL

You will need to begin this recipe 1 day ahead.

Drain and rinse the soaked dal and kidney beans, put in a large heavy-based saucepan over medium heat and cover with about 4 cm (1½ inches) of water. As soon as it comes to the boil, reduce the heat to as low as possible and cook for about 2 hours or until the lentils and beans are tender, adding a little more water if it is looking dry.

When the lentils are cooked, add the tomato, butter, ginger and garlic and cook for 20 minutes. The secret to a good dal is cooking over low heat over a long period.

Heat the oil in a small frying pan over medium heat, add the cumin seeds and when they turn semi-brown, add the onion and chilli powder and cook, stirring regularly, for 8 minutes. This is the tempering.

When the dal is cooked, add the hot tempering, season with salt, mix gently to combine and cook for 5 minutes. The colour should be dark brown.

Ladle into bowls, add a tomato half to each bowl, drizzle with a little cream and scatter over some ginger and coriander. For extra richness, add a small knob of butter to each bowl.

Tip: Let the lentils soak overnight to save on preparation time. It's important to use dried and not tinned kidney beans, as tinned beans do not give the desired starchy texture to the dish.

rasam

tomato, pepper & tamarind soup

There is an old Indian saying, 'education begins at home', and this was the very first dish I learned from my grandma when I was eight years old. It is one of the most simple dishes to make, but as with most simple dishes, the flavours must be balanced well and timing is key. The secret is to cook it for the right amount of time and keep the flavours lingering on the tongue. Rasam is an everyday dish eaten with only white rice, accompanied with other vegetables or meat. It is cooked in two stages. The first stage is with the tamarind and tomato where everything is cooked to boiling point to make a concentrated mix. The second stage is when the cooked dal is added with water, but not allowed to boil — it should only simmer. The finished dish is a thin broth.

70 g (2½ oz/⅓ cup) toor dal (yellow lentils) (see glossary)

¼ teaspoon ground turmeric

1 teaspoon vegetable oil

½ teaspoon black mustard seeds

1 teaspoon cumin seeds

¼ teaspoon asafoetida (see glossary)

3 garlic cloves, crushed

1½ tablespoons rasam powder (see page 215)

3 tablespoons tamarind pulp (see glossary)

2 ripe tomatoes, chopped

1 bunch coriander (cilantro), leaves finely chopped and stalks tied together with string

juice of 1 lime

1 teaspoon ghee (see glossary)

1–2 dried red chillies

10 curry leaves

SERVES 6 AS PART OF A SHARED MEAL

Put the dal in a heavy-based saucepan with 1.5 litres (52 fl oz) of water and the turmeric. Bring to the boil, then simmer for 30–40 minutes or until soft. (Indian housewives generally cook this dal in a pressure cooker.) Set aside in the cooking water, do not drain.

Heat the oil in a heavy-based saucepan, add ¼ teaspoon of the mustard seeds and let them crackle. Then add ½ teaspoon of the cumin seeds and all of the asafoetida and lightly brown the cumin, stirring regularly. Add the garlic and stir for 1 minute. Add 750 ml (26 fl oz/3 cups) of water, the rasam powder, tamarind pulp, tomato and coriander stalks, bring to the boil and cook for 15 minutes. This will infuse all of the flavours together. Season with salt.

Once boiled, add the dal and the cooking water and simmer for 5 minutes — do not allow it to boil. Remove the coriander stalks and stir in the coriander leaves and lime juice. Remove from the heat.

To make the tempering, heat the ghee in a small frying pan over medium–high heat, add the dried chillies and the remaining ¼ teaspoon mustard seeds and let them crackle. Add the remaining ½ teaspoon cumin seeds and let them brown. Add the curry leaves, then stir the mixture through the cooked rasam. Immediately cover with a lid and leave for 5 minutes. This is important as the tempering will seep through the rasam to flavour it. Check the seasoning, adding some black pepper to taste. Ladle into bowls to serve.

potato karakari

spicy fried potato

This dish is an essential accompaniment to a Tamil meal, enjoyed by people from all walks of life. My son Akilesh is very fond of it. This has always been the case except for one occasion when he was about ten years old. He wanted to help me in the kitchen, so I had him peel a bag of potatoes for an Abhi's anniversary dinner in which we were serving the karakari. I think the sheer quantity of potatoes he had to peel turned him off karakari for a while ... Well, at least on that occasion he did not eat any! I prefer to use kipflers, which don't need peeling — just give them a good scrub.

800 g (1 lb 12 oz) kipfler potatoes, scrubbed well and quartered lengthways

1½ teaspoons ground turmeric

3 tablespoons vegetable or sunflower oil

¼ teaspoon black mustard seeds

1 teaspoon split urad dal (split black lentils/black gram) (see glossary)

1 teaspoon split chana dal (see glossary)

2 dried red chillies, seeds removed and sliced

⅛ teaspoon asafoetida (see glossary)

2 onions, thinly sliced

2 teaspoons sweet paprika

2 teaspoons coriander seeds, crushed

10 curry leaves

SERVES 6 AS PART OF A SHARED MEAL

Put the potato in a saucepan of water with ½ teaspoon of the turmeric, bring to the boil, then cook for 10–15 minutes or until just tender. Drain and cool.

Heat the oil in a wok over medium heat, add the mustard seeds and let them crackle for about 20 seconds. Add the urad and chana dal and fry until golden brown. Add the chilli and asafoetida and cook for 1 minute.

Add the onion and cook over low heat until softened — do not brown.

Add the cooked potato, paprika, coriander seeds, remaining turmeric and 3 tablespoons of water and cook, covered, over low heat for 5 minutes — the water assists in the spices coating the potatoes. Check the seasoning, then stir in the curry leaves and serve.

vazhakai thoran

green banana & coconut

There is an interesting saying in Tamil, 'vazai pol vazhu' — live like a banana tree. The nature of the banana tree is always giving and sharing. Every part of the tree is used in some form or other. Fibre from the banana plant is used as thread to weave garlands. Banana leaves are used as disposable plates in Southern India because when hot food is served on them the vitamins and minerals in the leaves are released — one has to experience eating on a banana leaf to know how it enhances the flavour of a dish. The banana stem and its flowers are also used in dishes that are eaten to remove kidney stones.

The banana tree is a symbol of fertility — even before a plant dies a new shoot emerges. Tamil Brahmins have a great affinity for the banana plant, and raw banana features in almost all the major occasions in a Tamil Brahmin household: birth, mourning and festivities, including New Year. The recipe below is a variation on the standard, as a strict Brahmin would not use onion or garlic.

6 green bananas

3 tablespoons coconut oil

¼ teaspoon black mustard seeds

1 teaspoon split urad dal
(black lentils/black gram)
(see glossary)

1 teaspoon split chana dal
(see glossary)

6 garlic cloves, crushed

2 dried red chillies, seeds removed
and thinly sliced

¼ teaspoon ground turmeric

⅛ teaspoon asafoetida
(see glossary)

4 French shallots (eschalots),
thinly sliced

40 g (1½ oz/⅓ cup) grated coconut
(see glossary) or 30 g (1 oz/⅓ cup)
desiccated coconut

10 curry leaves

SERVES 4–6 AS PART OF A SHARED MEAL

Peel the bananas and slice into bite-sized pieces.

Heat the oil in a wok over medium heat. Add the mustard seeds and let them crackle for about 20 seconds. Add the urad and chana dal and fry for 3–4 minutes or until golden brown. Add the garlic, red chilli, turmeric and asafoetida and cook for 1 minute. Add the shallot and cook until softened — do not brown. Add the raw banana and cook, covered, for 5 minutes.

Finally, stir in the coconut and curry leaves, check the seasoning and serve.

vellai porrial

cauliflower & coconut

In Tamil 'vellai' means white. This dish is as appealing visually as it is delicious to eat. The white cauliflower and beans with freshly grated coconut are beautifully balanced with the curry leaves, both for colour and flavour and are complemented by the sweetness of the shallot. The heat of the green and red chillies completes this fabulous dish.

600 g (1 lb 5 oz) cauliflower florets

100 g (3½ oz) double-peeled broad (fava) beans

3 tablespoons gingili (unscented sesame oil) (see glossary)

¼ teaspoon black mustard seeds

⅛ teaspoon asafoetida (see glossary)

1 teaspoon split urad dal (black lentils/black gram) (see glossary)

1 teaspoon split chana dal (see glossary)

2 dried red chillies, halved lengthways and seeds removed

2 green chillies, seeds removed and finely shredded

4 French shallots (eschalots), thinly sliced

40 g (1½ oz/⅓ cup) grated coconut (see glossary) or 30 g (1 oz/⅓ cup) desiccated coconut

fried curry leaves, to garnish

SERVES 4 AS PART OF A SHARED MEAL

Cook the cauliflower in 1 litre (35 fl oz/4 cups) of salted boiling water for 5–7 minutes. Remove with a slotted spoon and set aside to cool.

Allow the water to come back to the boil, then add the broad beans and cook for 3–4 minutes. Drain and set aside.

Heat the gingili in a wok over medium heat, add the mustard seeds and asafoetida and let the mustard seeds crackle for about 20 seconds. Add the urad and chana dal and fry until golden brown. Add the red and green chillies and cook for 1 minute.

Add the shallot and sweat for 4–5 minutes or until softened — do not brown.

Add the cauliflower and broad beans and cook, covered, for 5 minutes to allow the spices to infuse the vegetables.

Finally, stir in the coconut, check the seasoning and garnish with the fried curry leaves.

amma's dosa

spiced rice pancake

A dish originating with my grandma, fed to me by my mum as a child and still fed to me by my wife. The tradition continues! I hope to train my future daughters-in-law to make it as well (mastery of this dish is a prerequisite for my sons' marriage too). It is a simple preparation that can be conjured up in minutes. It is a fuss-free snack for the evening 'tiffin'.

95 g (3¼ oz/½ cup) fine semolina

3 tablespoons rice flour

3 tablespoons plain (all-purpose) flour

3 tablespoons buttermilk

ghee (see glossary), for cooking

store-bought lime pickle, to serve

tomato chilli chutney (see page 108), to serve (optional)

TEMPERING

1 tablespoon gingili (unscented sesame oil) (see glossary)

½ teaspoon black mustard seeds

1 teaspoon cumin seeds

¼ teaspoon chilli flakes

2 small green chillies, chopped

⅛ teaspoon asafoetida (see glossary)

10 curry leaves, finely shredded

MAKES ABOUT 15

Combine the semolina, rice flour and plain flour in a large bowl with the buttermilk and 435 ml (15¼ fl oz/1¾ cups) of water and stir to combine until smooth. Set aside.

To make the tempering, heat the gingili in a small frying pan over medium–high heat, add the mustard seeds and let them crackle for 20 seconds. Add the cumin, chilli flakes, green chilli and asafoetida and cook for less than 1 minute. Remove from the heat and add the curry leaves. Stir the tempering into the semolina batter.

Heat a little ghee in an omelette or similar-sized frying pan over medium–high heat. Whisk the batter to combine again, then put 2 tablespoons of batter into the pan and swirl the mixture around to make a very thin pancake about 12.5 cm (5 inches) in diameter. Cook for 1 minute, then carefully flip over and cook for 30 seconds. Transfer to a plate while you make the remaining dosa, stirring the batter each time before adding it to the pan.

Serve immediately with the lime pickle and chutney.

Tip: This is an unfermented dosa batter and is not supposed to be a crispy dosa. The mixture should be more like a crepe batter.

Most Indian meals are cooked then tempered with either black mustard seeds, cumin seeds, urad dal (black lentils/black gram) and/or chillies in gingili or ghee. The critical part of tempering is not to burn or overcook the tempering and to retain the flavour and colour of each ingredient. This is then added to the dish at the finishing stage and usually immediately covered so the flavours can infuse the dish.

dal & spinach massial

lentil & spinach curry

This is a healthy dish with high iron and protein content from the spinach and lentils. 'Massial' denotes a dish that is a near mushed consistency, but not a purée. I have childhood memories of mashing the preparation for my mum in the kitchen with a wooden mallet. This dish was traditionally cooked in a black stone pot (makkal chatty).

3 tablespoons toor dal (yellow lentils) (see glossary), rinsed

30 ml (1 fl oz) vegetable or sunflower oil

½ teaspoon black mustard seeds

¼ teaspoon asafoetida (see glossary)

2 dried red chillies

2 bunches English spinach, chopped

10 curry leaves

2 teaspoons finely grated ginger

½ teaspoon crushed garlic

3 small green chillies

1 tomato, diced

SERVES 4 AS PART OF A SHARED MEAL

Put the dal in a large heavy-based saucepan, cover with about 4 cm (1½ inches) of water and bring to the boil over medium heat. As soon as it comes to the boil, reduce the heat to as low as possible and cook, covered, for 45 minutes or until tender, adding a little more water if it is looking dry. Set aside.

Heat the oil in a large wok — this is necessary as the chopped spinach is fairly voluminous but it will shrink on cooking — over medium–high heat, add the mustard seeds and let them crackle for about 20 seconds. Add the asafoetida and the dried chillies and cook for about 2 minutes or until the chillies are lightly browned.

Add the remaining ingredients (except the dal), season with salt and cook, covered, over medium heat until the spinach is cooked — do not add any water as the spinach will wilt and release enough water. Once the spinach is cooked, stir in the cooked dal and serve hot.

tirunelveli varutha kozhi

aromatic chicken curry

My hometown of Tirunelveli in the southernmost part of India inspired this recipe. Tirunelveli is located in a region formerly known as Nanjilnadu, ranging from Madurai to Kanyakumari, and the main spices used there are coriander seeds and ginger. This dish is finished off with crushed coriander seeds and cumin, which add a unique freshness to the curry. It is a light yet aromatic curry.

800 g (1 lb 12 oz) skinless, boneless chicken thigh fillets, diced

½ teaspoon ground turmeric

1 teaspoon cumin seeds

100 ml (3½ fl oz) vegetable or sunflower oil

½ teaspoon fennel seeds

4 dried red chillies

5 cm (2 inch) piece of cassia bark (see glossary)

6 green cardamom pods

1 dried bay leaf

6 garlic cloves, sliced

1 large onion, sliced

1½ teaspoons finely grated ginger

2 tomatoes, chopped

10 curry leaves

1 tablespoon coriander seeds, crushed

½ teaspoon South Indian garam masala (see glossary)

½ bunch coriander (cilantro), leaves chopped

SERVES 6–8 AS PART OF A SHARED MEAL

Rub the chicken with the turmeric and set aside.

Meanwhile, heat a small frying pan over high heat and dry-fry the cumin seeds for about 1 minute, shaking the pan regularly. Finely crush the seeds using a mortar and pestle.

Heat 80 ml (2½ fl oz/⅓ cup) of the oil in a large heavy-based frying pan over medium–high heat, add the fennel seeds, dried chillies, cassia bark, cardamom, bay leaf and garlic and cook for 1 minute.

Add the onion and cook for 6–8 minutes or until browned.

Add the ginger and chicken and stir to coat the chicken. Cook for about 5 minutes. Add the tomato and cook for about 10 minutes or until the chicken is nearly cooked through.

Meanwhile, heat the remaining oil in a small frying pan over medium–high heat, add the curry leaves and fry for about 30 seconds. Drain on paper towel.

Add the crushed cumin seeds, crushed coriander seeds, garam masala, curry leaves and chopped coriander to the chicken mixture and stir to combine. Season with salt and serve.

flathead pakoras

fish fritters

juice of 1 lime

½ teaspoon ground turmeric

½ teaspoon ground cumin

2 teaspoons finely grated ginger

4 garlic cloves, crushed

800 g (1 lb 12 oz) flathead fillets,
each cut into 3 pieces

60 g (2¼ oz/½ cup) chickpea
flour (besan)

3 tablespoons rice flour

2 teaspoons coriander seeds,
finely crushed

½ teaspoon red chilli powder

vegetable or sunflower oil,
for deep-frying

¼ pomegranate, seeds removed

fennel fronds, to garnish (optional)

green chutney (see page 210),
to serve

SERVES 4 AS PART OF A SHARED MEAL

Combine the lime juice, turmeric, cumin, ginger and garlic, rub all over the fish and set aside for 20 minutes.

Meanwhile, combine the chickpea and rice flours with the crushed coriander seeds and chilli powder in a flat container. Roll the fish in the spiced flour mixture.

Fill a wok or heavy-based saucepan one-third full with oil and heat to 180°C (356°F) or until a cube of bread turns golden brown in 15 seconds. Deep-fry the fish for 4–5 minutes or until golden brown. Remove with a slotted spoon and drain on paper towel.

Serve garnished with the pomegranate seeds and fennel fronds, and accompanied by the green chutney.

jackfruit payasam

rice pudding

This was my grandma's favourite dessert. The original dish strictly uses fresh jackfruit but we can make our life much, much easier using the tinned version. Fresh jackfruit is messy as it secretes a resin that sticks like super glue, and handling it requires a lot of technique. My gran's trick was to apply coconut oil to her hands before touching the jackfruit. The seed of the jackfruit is also a popular snack, consumed like chestnuts.

40 g (1½ oz) basmati rice

2 teaspoons ghee (see glossary)

2 teaspoons unsalted cashew nuts, roughly chopped

5 saffron threads

3 teaspoons rosewater

1 litre (35 fl oz/4 cups) milk

4 green cardamom pods, crushed

100 g (3½ oz) white sugar

50 g (1¾ oz) tinned jackfruit, finely chopped

sultanas (golden raisins), to garnish

SERVES 6 AS A DESSERT

Soak the rice in cold water for 30 minutes, then drain.

Heat the ghee in a small saucepan over medium–high heat and fry the cashew nuts for about 1 minute, shaking the pan regularly.

Soak the saffron threads in the rosewater to make a saffron water. Set aside.

Put the milk and cardamom pods in a heavy-based saucepan over low heat and simmer, uncovered, for about 20 minutes. Add the rice and cook, uncovered, for 30 minutes or until the rice is soft.

Add the sugar and jackfruit and cook for 10–15 minutes.

Once it has thickened slightly, add the saffron water, remove from the heat and cool slightly. It is supposed to be liquidy.

Divide among individual glasses or serving dishes and serve warm or cold garnished with the fried cashew nuts and sultanas.

Tip: Be patient and cook over low heat.

beetroot halwa

sweet beetroot pudding

Traditionally halwa is eaten in Northern India during winter, where it is made using the red carrots that the region is famous for, while in Southern India, they eat a beetroot version all year round.

500 g (1 lb 2 oz) beetroot (beets), washed and grated

500 ml (17 fl oz/2 cups) milk

125 g (4½ oz) white sugar

50 g (¾ oz) ghee (see glossary)

½ teaspoon ground cardamom

1 tablespoon raisins, lightly crushed using a mortar and pestle

2 tablespoons pistachio nuts, roughly chopped

strawberry coulis (see page 162), edible silver leaf, rose petal ice cream and edible flowers, to serve (optional)

SERVES 4 AS A DESSERT

Put the beetroot in a saucepan with the milk and 125 ml (4 fl oz/ ½ cup) of water and cook over low heat for 20 minutes or until the beetroot softens and most of the liquid has been absorbed.

Add the sugar, mix well and cook for about 30 minutes or until the sugar has dissolved and all the milk has been absorbed.

Add 30 g (1 oz) of the ghee, the cardamom and raisins, mix well and simmer for 2–3 minutes. Remove from the heat and set aside.

Heat the remaining ghee in a small frying pan over medium heat and fry the pistachio nuts until lightly golden.

Serve the halwa hot, cold or at room temperature in a bowl or form into small quenelles (oval mounds). Drizzle with the strawberry coulis, garnish with silver leaf and serve with rose petal ice cream, the fried nuts and edible flowers if desired.

Tip: Make sure that all the beetroot has been cooked and there is very little water left before adding the sugar.

bitter

BITTERNESS IS NECESSARY TO BALANCE not only flavour but the struggles and realities of life. This was a lesson I learned early when I decided to become a chef and not a doctor as my parents had hoped. That was a big shock to my parents, despite me showing so much interest in cooking with my grandma. Truth is always bitter. Being raised a strict Brahmin, in which the consumption of meat or seafood is a sin, my family were completely against my chosen path of study and believed I was disrespecting my culture and traditions. It was an immense struggle to make them understand my new path of study, but my decision to become a chef was fuelled with the good intention to feed people beautiful food.

From a young age, my parents taught me a saying: 'Annadhatha Sukhibhava', which means, 'God bless the provider of food'. It is a way to express gratitude to one who provides or serves food and using this line of reasoning that serving food is as sacred as being a devout Brahmin my parents finally relinquished. Looking back, this clash with my parents was necessary to balance out all the good fortune to come …

Bitterness is one of the six rasas, or flavours, alongside salty, astringent, sour, pungent and sweet, which form the basis for every meal. Indians believe that bitterness is necessary in life to balance the system. Bitter foods often have a high medicinal value, while bitter vegetables and spices can enhance the other flavours in a dish.

Spices such as turmeric, cumin and fenugreek also have bitter characteristics. While cumin seeds are slightly bitter, they add a sweet aroma to dishes. Ground turmeric is highly regarded for stomach and liver ailments, as well as treating cuts or wounds, while anyone with a sore throat is advised to drink milk with turmeric. Turmeric is also an excellent preservative, which is why it's used extensively in Indian pickles.

Fenugreek is the most interestingly and distinctively bitter spice. Its medicinal qualities have been recognised since ancient times. Among its many attributes, the one people will appreciate most is its ability to reduce flatulence. The young leaves, called methi, can be used in salads. Most importantly, fenugreek is an important base note in curries. It's one of those essential scents that help you recognise Indian food.

And so it is in life too. Without the bitter struggles of my early years, I would not have recognised that being a chef was exactly what I was supposed to be.

karela masala

bitter melon curry

Bitter melon, known as karela in India, is a climbing vine with bitter leaves and green fruit. A key part of Indian cooking, it's used to cut the fattiness in food as well as providing a contrast to richer flavours. It has Ayurvedic qualities that Indians believe are beneficial in dealing with diabetes and many infectious diseases as well as having a positive effect on the metabolism. Every state has its own bitter melon recipe; this dish is from North India. The baby bitter melons are split then salted to remove some of the bitterness, then stuffed with spices and slowly roasted with ginger. This is probably our family's most favourite dish. It is an excellent blend of flavours and encompasses the five tastes: bitter from the bitter melon itself, sour from the dry mango powder 'amchur', spice from the red chilli and turmeric, sweet from the jaggery and salt for balance. The bitter melon is treated properly prior to cooking to cut down its inherent bitterness. The salt, amchur and lime juice work to reduce the bitterness of the melon.

600 g (1 lb 5 oz) bitter melon

1 teaspoon ground turmeric

juice of 1 lime

vegetable or sunflower oil, for cooking

2 red onions, thinly sliced

60 g (2¼ oz/½ cup) chickpea flour (besan)

1 teaspoon cumin seeds

¼ teaspoon asafoetida (see glossary)

½ teaspoon red chilli powder

4 small green chillies, chopped

2 teaspoons grated palm sugar (jaggery) or soft brown sugar

¼ teaspoon amchur (dry mango powder) (see glossary)

coriander (cilantro) leaves, to garnish

SERVES 6 AS PART OF A SHARED MEAL

Cut the bitter melon in half, remove the insides and discard them. Cut the flesh into 1–2 cm (½–¾ inch) thick rounds and put in a colander. Add ½ teaspoon of the turmeric, ½ teaspoon of salt and the lime juice to the bitter melon. Leave in the colander over a plate, as the melon will release some water, for 20 minutes. (You can discard this water but it is also used in India as a medicine to control diabetes.)

Fill a wok or heavy-based saucepan one-third full with oil and heat to 180°C (356°F) or until a cube of bread turns golden brown in 15 seconds. Deep-fry half of the onion until crisp. Remove with a slotted spoon and drain on paper towel. Set aside. These will be used to finish the dish.

Ensure the oil in the wok is still at 180°C. Roll the bitter melon in the chickpea flour and deep-fry for 3–4 minutes or until golden. Remove with a slotted spoon and drain on paper towel. Set aside.

Heat 3 tablespoons of oil in a large frying pan over medium heat, add the cumin seeds and brown. Add the remaining uncooked onion and cook until brown. Add the asafoetida, chilli powder, green chilli and palm sugar and cook for 3 minutes, sprinkling with a little bit of water to prevent the mixture burning.

Add the bitter melon crisps and toss quickly. Sprinkle with the amchur and garnish with the coriander leaves and fried onion.

chicken 65

This dish originated in a famous eatery in Chennai called Buhari. The true origin of the '65' is highly debated. According to the most prevalent theory, it was the 65th item on a long menu, but another common anecdote is that the dish uses a chicken that has been reared for 65 days.

1 tablespoon finely grated ginger

1 tablespoon crushed garlic

1½ tablespoons red chilli powder

juice of 1½ limes

3 eggs, lightly beaten

700 g (1 lb 9 oz) skinless chicken thigh fillets, cut into bite-sized pieces

3 tablespoons plain (all-purpose) flour

vegetable or sunflower oil, for deep-frying

20 curry leaves

finely shredded ginger, to garnish

green chutney (see page 210), to serve (optional)

SERVES 4 AS PART OF A SHARED MEAL

Combine the finely grated ginger, garlic, chilli powder, lime juice and eggs in a shallow dish. Add the chicken and mix well. Leave to marinate in the fridge for 30 minutes. The longer you allow the chicken to marinate, the more the flavours will infuse into the chicken.

Remove the chicken from the marinade, allowing any excess to drip off. Dust the chicken lightly with the flour.

Fill a wok or heavy-based saucepan one-third full with oil and heat to 180°C (356°F) or until a cube of bread turns golden brown in 15 seconds. Deep-fry the chicken for about 3 minutes or until golden brown and cooked through. Remove with a slotted spoon and drain on paper towel. Put in a serving dish.

In the same oil, deep-fry the curry leaves until crispy — this will happen very quickly, about 20 seconds. Remove with a slotted spoon and drain on paper towel.

Crush half of the fried curry leaves and scatter over the fried chicken. Garnish the chicken with the remaining fried curry leaves and the ginger and serve with the chutney.

thengai erachi

beef chilli coconut fry

This dish is from the Syrian Christian community in the South Indian state of Kerala. The coconut with fennel and the garam masala and pepper work well together. The beef is a robust enough meat to stand up to the strong spices. The cooking medium is coconut oil, which is found in abundance in this region of India. Keralan cuisine uses the coconut as well as a lot of spice as the region has been a major spice trader centre for centuries.

½ teaspoon ground turmeric

2 teaspoons ground coriander

1 teaspoon ground cumin

½ teaspoon ground fennel

½ teaspoon South Indian garam masala (see glossary)

600 g (1 lb 5 oz) beef sirloin or rump steak, cut into finger-sized strips

2 tablespoons vegetable oil

6 curry leaves

100 ml (3½ fl oz) coconut oil (see glossary)

4 dried red chillies

5 cm (2 inch) piece of cassia bark (see glossary)

1 large onion, sliced

6 garlic cloves, sliced

½ teaspoon cracked black pepper

1½ teaspoons finely grated ginger

3 tablespoons coconut flakes or desiccated coconut, toasted

SERVES 4–6 AS PART OF A SHARED MEAL

Combine the turmeric, coriander, cumin, fennel and garam masala in a bowl. Add the beef and toss to coat in the spices. Set aside to marinate for 30 minutes.

Heat the oil in a frying pan over low heat, add the curry leaves and fry until just crisp. Drain on paper towel and set aside.

Heat 3 tablespoons of the coconut oil in a wok over medium heat, add the chillies and cassia bark and cook for 1 minute. Add the onion and cook for 5 minutes or until softened. Add the garlic and pepper and cook for 1 minute. Add the ginger and cook for 1 minute.

Heat the remaining coconut oil in a separate large frying pan over high heat and seal the beef, in two batches. This is to prevent the beef from releasing too much moisture.

Once all the beef is cooked, add it to the wok, with the coconut flakes and fried curry leaves. Mix quickly, season with salt and serve.

kothu kari

stir-fried chopped lamb

*Kothu in Tamil means 'chopped'. The technique uses
two cleavers, one in each hand to chop the meat.*

600 g (1 lb 5 oz) lamb shoulder

200 g (7 oz) lamb backstrap

**100 ml (3½ fl oz) vegetable
or sunflower oil**

1 teaspoon black mustard seeds

2 onions, chopped

1 tablespoon finely grated ginger

1 tablespoon crushed garlic

1 teaspoon ground fennel

**2 teaspoons ground
black pepper**

1 teaspoon ground turmeric

2 teaspoons red chilli powder

1 tablespoon ground coriander

juice of 1 lime

10 curry leaves

SERVES 4–6 AS PART OF A SHARED MEAL

Put both cuts of lamb on a chopping board and, using two
cleavers, dice into 1–2 cm (½–¾ inch) cubes using a chopping
action. The diced meat should be chopped but not minced.

Heat 2 tablespoons of the oil in a large wok over high heat,
add the lamb, in batches, and stir-fry for 1 minute. Remove from
the wok and set aside.

Heat the remaining oil in the wok, add the mustard seeds and
let them crackle for about 20 seconds. Add the onion, ginger and
garlic and stir-fry for about 3 minutes or until lightly browned.

Return the lamb to the wok, then stir in the fennel, pepper,
turmeric, chilli powder and coriander and stir-fry until the meat is
cooked. Drizzle over the lime juice, stir in the curry leaves and serve.

chicken harra masala

coriander & mint chicken

A North Indian favourite, with the freshness of green herbs and background notes of spices.
These make the dish very fresh, light and crisp in taste. The 'harra' refers to the colour meaning green.
It's best to cook the dish without a lid, which will help to retain the colour.

**vegetable or sunflower oil,
for deep-frying**

3 onions, thinly sliced

8 small green chillies

1 bunch mint, leaves picked

**1 bunch coriander (cilantro),
leaves picked**

50 g (1¾ oz/⅓ cup) cashew nuts

**130 g (4½ oz/½ cup) plain
thick yoghurt, beaten**

2 teaspoons finely grated ginger

2 teaspoons crushed garlic

**1 kg (2 lb 4 oz) skinless, boneless
chicken thigh fillets, cut into
4 cm (1½ inch) pieces**

**2.5 cm (1 inch) piece of
cinnamon stick**

4 green cardamom pods

8 black peppercorns

1 teaspoon cumin seeds

2 teaspoons coriander seeds

**3 tablespoons ghee
(see glossary)**

¼ teaspoon ground turmeric

**2 tablespoons thin
(pouring) cream**

**cherry tomato quarters and ginger
slices, to garnish**

SERVES 6–8 AS PART OF A SHARED MEAL

Fill a wok or heavy-based saucepan one-third full with oil and heat to 180°C (356°F) or until a cube of bread turns golden brown in 15 seconds. Deep-fry the onion until crisp. Remove with a slotted spoon and drain on paper towel. Reserve some to garnish.

Grind the green chillies, mint leaves, coriander leaves, cashew nuts and remaining fried onion together in a food processor to make a smooth paste. This is your green masala.

Combine the yoghurt, ginger, garlic and green masala in a large bowl. Add the chicken and mix well to coat. Leave to marinate in the fridge for 30 minutes.

Meanwhile, put the cinnamon, cardamom, peppercorns, and cumin and coriander seeds in a spice grinder and grind to a fine powder. This is your powdered masala. Set aside.

Heat the ghee in a large frying pan over medium–high heat, add the chicken and seal on all sides. Add the turmeric, 250 ml (9 fl oz/1 cup) of water and season with salt. Cook, uncovered, for about 15 minutes.

When the chicken is almost cooked, add the powdered masala and cream and simmer for 5 minutes or until the chicken is cooked through and the sauce is smooth and rich. Ladle into a serving dish and garnish with the reserved fried onions, cherry tomato and ginger.

rajastani laal maas

fiery goat curry

This is a very spicy dish from the deserts of Rajasthan. It's marked by a striking red colour from the chillies. A chilli paste is made from soaked whole chillies, which gives it a very different taste from red chilli powder. Also, ghee is used instead of oil to balance the heat of the chillies. This dish is unusual as it does not use ginger or tomato.

20 dried red chillies

1 teaspoon cumin seeds

130 g (4½ oz/½ cup) Greek-style yoghurt

½ teaspoon ground turmeric

2 tablespoons ground coriander

100 g (3½ oz) ghee (see glossary)

6 garlic cloves, sliced

6 green cardamom pods

3 black cardamom pods

2 onions, thinly sliced

1.25 kg (2 lb 12 oz) goat leg or shoulder shank, bone in, cubed (ask your butcher to do this for you)

SERVES 6 AS PART OF A SHARED MEAL

Soak the dried chillies in warm water for 20 minutes to soften. Drain and reserve 4 chillies for later. Process the remainder to a fine paste in a blender.

Heat a frying pan over high heat and dry-fry the cumin seeds for about 1 minute, shaking the pan regularly. Finely crush the seeds using a mortar and pestle.

Combine the yoghurt with the turmeric, ground coriander, chilli paste and crushed cumin seeds in a bowl and set aside.

Heat the ghee in a large heavy-based saucepan over medium–high heat, add the garlic and cook for 2 minutes or until golden brown. Add the green and black cardamom pods and the reserved chillies, stir, then add the onion and cook for 6–8 minutes or until brown.

Add the goat and cook for 4–5 minutes, stirring to coat in the onion. Add the yoghurt mixture with 750 ml (26 fl oz/3 cups) of water, bring to the boil, then reduce the heat to low and cook, uncovered, stirring occasionally, for about 2 hours or until the meat is tender. Check the seasoning and serve hot.

ponnusamy biryani

spiced rice with lamb

My addiction to biryani started from my catering college days in Madras when I discovered Ponnusamy Hotel. This small no-frills eatery now has a legendary status. It started in 1954 and serves one of the best biryanis in town. The rice used here is a special variety called seeraga samba, which has a beautiful bouquet that lends itself to a good biryani. There are a vast number of biryani recipes in India, varying from region to region and even from home to home — and each region boasts that their version is the greatest.

Biryani is derived from the Persian word 'biran' which means 'fried before cooking'. There are primarily two ways to cook a biryani. The first style is a kachi (raw) biryani, where the meat and rice are sealed and slow-cooked in 'dum' (together) for hours in a traditional pot called a lagan. This involves a lot of technique and is usually done by ustaads (master chefs), who have their chelas (apprentices or servants) to do all their prep and rice washing. The chelas are not allowed to open the biryani because the master believes if they do, they can break the grains. The ustaad would generally share his secret recipes with only his family or a select deputy. This biryani is a speciality of the city of Hyderabad. I was lucky enough to receive a demonstration from legendary chef Maqbul Miaji of Hyderabad.

Pukki (cooked) biryani is the less involved method where the meat and rice are par-cooked separately and then the rice is layered on the meat, and the whole pot is sealed and cooked together. I was amazed to see a biryani master in Lucknow making a pukki biryani for about a thousand people in ten huge lagans cooked over fires. His presicion and timing left me in awe.

This recipe is a simplified pukki biryani.

80 ml (2½ fl oz/⅓ cup) vegetable or sunflower oil

6 green cardamom pods

2 cinnamon sticks

4 whole cloves

2 dried bay leaves

3 onions, sliced

1 tablespoon finely grated ginger

2 teaspoons crushed garlic

1 kg (2 lb 4 oz) lamb leg, diced

2 lamb shanks, cut into 5 cm (2 inch) rounds (ask your butcher to do this)

95 g (3¼ oz/⅓ cup) plain thick yoghurt, beaten

1 tomato, chopped

½ bunch coriander (cilantro), leaves roughly chopped and stalks reserved

¼ bunch mint, leaves roughly chopped

½ teaspoon ground turmeric

2 teaspoons Kashmiri chilli powder (see glossary)

1 teaspoon red chilli powder

500 g (1 lb 2 oz/2½ cups) basmati rice

½ teaspoon garam masala

5 saffron threads

3 tablespoons ghee (see glossary), melted

100 g (3½ oz) butter, melted

3 tablespoons thin (pouring) cream

fried onions and fried green chillies, to garnish

SERVES 6–8 AS PART OF A SHARED MEAL

Heat the oil in a casserole dish over medium heat, add 4 of the cardamom pods, 1 cinnamon stick, 2 cloves and the bay leaves. Add the onion and cook for 6–8 minutes or until golden brown. Add the ginger and garlic and cook for 2–3 minutes. Add the lamb, season with salt and cook, covered, for about 5 minutes or until the lamb starts to release its juices.

Stir in the yoghurt and tomato. Add 250 ml (9 fl oz/1 cup) of water, bring to the boil, then reduce the heat to low and cook for 30 minutes. Add half of the coriander leaves and one-third of the mint. Add the turmeric and both chilli powders and cook for 15 minutes or until the lamb is half-cooked. Season well with salt.

Preheat the oven to 180°C (350°F/Gas 4).

Meanwhile, fill a saucepan with 2 litres (70 fl oz) of water, add the remaining cardamom pods, cinnamon stick and cloves, one-third of the remaining mint and the coriander stalks and bring to the boil. Add the rice, season with salt and par-boil, uncovered, over medium–high heat for about 10 minutes. Do not drain.

When the meat is half-cooked, use a slotted spoon to constantly scoop small quantities of the rice onto the lamb, putting the rice in the centre of the meat — eventually you will have a mound of rice. Once all the rice has been added, flatten the mound slightly — not too much as you don't want the rice to get too soaked by the sauce. Do not stir the rice at any time from now — this is very important. Add the garam masala, saffron, ghee, butter and cream and the remaining mint and coriander leaves. Cover the dish with a wet cloth, then cover with a tight-fitting lid. The biryani must not be cooked over heat from this stage on. Transfer to the oven and cook for 15 minutes.

Remove the biryani from the oven, but do not open it to check whether it is done. Rest for 5–10 minutes to allow the flavours to develop. Garnish with the fried onion and green chillies to serve.

rava methi machi

semolina-crusted salmon

juice of 1 lime

1 teaspoon finely grated ginger

1 teaspoon crushed garlic

600 g (1 lb 5 oz) salmon fillets,
skin on, cut into 80–100 g
(2¾ oz/3½ oz) portions

95 g (3¼ oz/½ cup) coarse
semolina

3 tablespoons plain
(all-purpose) flour

1 tablespoon dried fenugreek
leaves (see glossary)

½ teaspoon ground cumin

¼ teaspoon ground turmeric

½ teaspoon red chilli powder

3 tablespoons vegetable
or sunflower oil

tamarind and ginger chutney
(see page 210), to serve

SERVES 6 AS PART OF A SHARED MEAL

Combine the lime juice, ginger and garlic, brush the mixture all over the salmon and set aside to marinate for 30 minutes.

Combine the semolina, flour, fenugreek leaves, cumin, turmeric and chilli powder. Heavily coat the salmon in the flour mixture.

Heat the oil in a large frying pan over medium–high heat, add the salmon, skin side down, and cook until the skin is crisp, then turn over and cook for a further 2–3 minutes or until the fish is just cooked through — do not overcook the salmon, it should be pink and soft in the middle. Serve with the tamarind and ginger chutney.

aatukal karaikudi

lamb karaikuidi

3 tablespoons vegetable or
sunflower oil

2 onions, roughly chopped

1 tablespoon coriander seeds

5 dried red chillies

½ teaspoon fennel seeds

2 star anise

1 tablespoon finely grated ginger

1 tablespoon crushed garlic

90 g (3¼ oz/⅓ cup) tomato paste
(concentrated purée)

1 kg (2 lb 4 oz) diced lamb leg

12 curry leaves

parathas (see glossary), to serve

Heat 1 tablespoon of the oil in a frying pan over medium heat, add the onion and coriander seeds and cook for 6–8 minutes or until the onion is brown. Cool, then put into a spice grinder and blend to a smooth paste.

Heat the remaining oil in a large saucepan over medium heat. Add the red chillies, fennel, star anise, ginger and garlic and cook for 2 minutes.

Add the onion paste and stir to combine well with the spices, then add the tomato paste and cook for 3 minutes.

Add the lamb and 500 ml (17 fl oz/2 cups) of water, reduce the heat to low and cook, covered, for 30 minutes. This dish should not have a flowing gravy, so if the sauce is still quite thin after cooking, increase the heat to high and cook, uncovered, for about 5 minutes or until the sauce has reduced to a thick consistency. Stir in the curry leaves and serve with the parathas.

karara bhindi

crispy okra

Okra are also called 'ladies' fingers' in India due to their curved shape. They are a rich source of dietary fibre, minerals and vitamins, and they are thought to enhance brain power. Prior to school exams okra is a prime vegetable that gets added to a lot of dishes — this is an ancient natural remedy that existed before such things as memory-boosting tablets came onto the market.

Okra is a naturally slimy vegetable that requires the right cooking technique, as shown in this recipe, to achieve the perfect texture and taste. These crispy snacks are an excellent accompaniment to a chilled beer on a summer afternoon. We serve this at Aki's as a starter.

500 g (1 lb 2 oz) okra, cut into strips

½ teaspoon red chilli powder

¼ teaspoon ground turmeric

juice of 1 lime

vegetable or sunflower oil, for deep-frying

120 g (4¼ oz / 1 cup) chickpea flour (besan)

80 g (2¾ oz / ½ cup) rice flour

½ teaspoon cumin seeds

2 teaspoons finely grated ginger

date and tamarind chutney (see page 108) or burrani raita (see page 211), to serve

SERVES 4 AS PART OF A SHARED MEAL

Lightly season the okra with the chilli powder, turmeric and lime juice. Do not marinate it for too long because the okra will leach its stickiness and make it very difficult to dust with the flour.

Fill a wok or large saucepan one-third full with oil and heat to about 180°C (356°F) or until a cube of bread turns golden brown in 15 seconds. Combine the chickpea and rice flours, cumin seeds, ginger and a little salt in a bowl. Dust the okra in the flour mixture. Deep-fry the okra, in batches, for 2–3 minutes or until golden brown and crisp, turning once to cook evenly. Remove with a slotted spoon and drain on paper towel. Serve immediately with the chutney or raita.

shahi tukda

mughal bread & butter pudding

This is essentially a glorified bread and butter pudding from the royal Mughal kitchens. The origin of this dish is Lucknow in Uttar Pradesh. In Urdu, shahi means 'royal' and tukda means 'bits' and refers to how the royal cooks would use the plethora of breads left over from the emperor's meals to prepare this dessert. This pudding is pure indulgence (and will ensure you need a couple of hours on the treadmill!). Traditionally to showcase the richness of Mughlai cuisine, chandi warq (edible silver leaf) is used to decorate dishes. This is still made in the traditional manner where small pieces of silver are placed between two sheets of paper and hammered out until it is papery thin. The silver leaf is pure fancy and adds to the opulence of the dish.

8 saffron threads

30 ml (1 fl oz) rosewater

500 ml (17 fl oz/2 cups) milk

6 slices white bread, crusts removed

125 g (4½ oz/½ cup) ghee (see glossary), melted

200 g (7 oz) white sugar

honey, for drizzling

1 sheet edible silver leaf (optional)

vanilla bean ice cream (optional), to serve

SERVES 6 AS A DESSERT

Preheat the oven to 180°C (350°F/Gas 4).

Soak 3 saffron threads in 25 ml (1 fl oz) of the rosewater to make a saffron rosewater for serving. Set aside.

Put the milk in a heavy-based stainless-steel saucepan and bring to the boil over low heat, stirring constantly. Continue gently simmering, scraping the sides and base of the pan to ensure the milk doesn't burn, until the milk has reduced to one-third. Set aside to cool. This is called the rabri.

Cut each slice of bread in half to make triangles and toast in the oven for 10 minutes, then brush each side with the melted ghee, return to the oven and toast for 15 minutes or until crisp and golden. Set aside.

Meanwhile, put the sugar in a saucepan with 400 ml (14 fl oz) of water, bring to the boil, then simmer for 10 minutes to make a syrup. Add the remaining saffron and the remaining rosewater. Remove from the heat.

Place the bread triangles in the hot sugar syrup and leave until well soaked.

To serve, arrange two bread triangles on each plate and pour over the rabri. Drizzle with the honey and the saffron rosewater. Using a knife, carefully remove a small piece of the silver leaf and put on each dish. Serve with a scoop of ice cream if desired.

sour

SOUR AWAKENS THE SPIRIT and sharpens the mind. Sourness sharpens flavours. It stimulates the tastebuds, and according to Ayurvedic beliefs it has a 'wake-up' quality, which brings us back to reality.

After I finished cooking college I landed a position at the Taj Mahal Palace Hotel in Bombay (now Mumbai). I was only seventeen and after the bitter struggle with my parents over my decision to become a chef, a job at a prestigious hotel in a big cosmopolitan city such as Bombay was exactly what I needed. It was my own 'wake-up' to reality, to forget the hardships I had endured to get there. My life was finally taking shape. The Taj was the first of many wake-up calls. I journeyed all over the subcontinent and further afield to the Sheraton in Iraq and was sent by the Indian government as a culinary ambassador to Australia. It was the 'sour' I had been looking for to balance the 'bitter'.

Sour foods are ideal for summer (along with salty, while in winter the flavours should shift to pungent and salty).

The original souring agents in Indian cooking were tamarind, green mango and kokam. They often act as preservatives and sourness plays an important part in pickling. Tamarind is an essential part of any Tamil fish curry, especially as people didn't have refrigeration in the past. Villagers would make their curry in a clay pot and the tamarind helped keep it fresh for a day or two — and as we all know, curry always tastes better the next day.

Kokam, which comes from the west coast and is part of the mangosteen family, has both medicinal and culinary uses and nearly all of the plant is used, mostly as a garnish for curries. You can find the fruit, oil and syrup in Australia. The fruit, which has a deep red beetroot colour, has a sweet, acidic taste (and antiseptic qualities) when fresh, but the flavour is tart when used dried, while the bark and leaves also have a more astringent flavour.

The gandhraj lemon is native to Kolkata (Calcutta) and has a distinct sour flavour I love.

When I sit down at the table, no meal is complete without a chutney or pickle. Chutneys and pickles are an excellent combination of sweet, sour, salty and sometimes chilli that brings everything alive and reinvigorates the palate. Mango pickles are an essential part of any meal. Green mango has a sour quality that provides an important contrast to the richness of a curry.

mango oysters

Every year in July we celebrate Abhi's anniversary with a new theme and food from a particular region of India. The reason for this is to take the customers on a tasty journey through the country's different regions. Travelling to various parts of India to discover the variety of food that exists has become a new tradition for both of us. Customers showed their interest in knowing about the differences in regional cooking and that encouraged us to broaden and deepen our knowledge of Indian food. The new discoveries made kept Abhi's moving in a direction of traditional yet contemporary Indian cuisine. This is one of the hits from an Abhi's anniversary dinner. This is a fresh and flavourful dressing with an Indian bent. It is quite versatile, try it on ceviche. The dressing can be made in advance.

1 green mango, peeled and finely diced

1 tablespoon amchur (dry mango powder) (see glossary) (optional) or 1 tablespoon lime juice

1 tablespoon finely grated ginger

2 tablespoons finely chopped coriander (cilantro), plus baby leaves to garnish

1 teaspoon white sugar

24 oysters, shucked and on the half shell

SERVES 4 AS A STARTER

You will need to begin this recipe 1 day ahead.

If the mango is not sour enough for your taste, sprinkle with the amchur. Put the mango in a bowl, add 1 teaspoon of salt and let it marinate in the fridge overnight. This will make the mango release its juices, which are quite acidic. Do not drain the juices.

Squeeze the juice from the ginger into a small bowl and discard the ginger. Add the coriander and sugar to the ginger juice and stir to dissolve the sugar.

Add to the mango. Spoon over the oysters and serve garnished with the baby coriander leaves.

brinjal mirchi salan

eggplant & chilli curry

A Hyderabadi (South Indian) delight. Hyderabad possesses a good fusion of Mughlai and Southern Indian cooking. The Nawabs of Hyderabad adapted the Mughlai cuisine to suit the region they found themselves in.

8 baby eggplants (aubergine)

1½ teaspoons ground turmeric

80 ml (2½ fl oz/⅓ cup) vegetable or sunflower oil

1 teaspoon panch phoran masala (see glossary)

2 red onions, thinly sliced

10 curry leaves

1 tablespoon finely grated ginger

2 teaspoons crushed garlic

2 tablespoons ground coriander

1½ tablespoons Kashmiri chilli powder (see glossary)

2 tablespoons tamarind pulp (see glossary)

2 long green capsicums (peppers), cut into 2.5 cm (1 inch) slices

fried curry leaves, to garnish

finely shredded ginger, to garnish

MASALA PASTE

50 g (1¾ oz/⅓ cup) raw peanuts, skins off

25 g (1 oz) sesame seeds

80 g (2¾ oz) desiccated coconut

4 small green chillies, chopped

SERVES 4–6 AS PART OF A SHARED MEAL

To make the masala paste, heat a medium frying pan over medium heat, add the peanuts, sesame seeds and coconut and dry-fry them until lightly toasted, shaking the pan regularly. Transfer to a small blender or spice grinder with the green chillies and process or grind to a smooth paste. Gradually add 125 ml (4 fl oz/½ cup) of water and process or grind until smooth and combined. Set aside.

Slice a deep cross in the base of each eggplant (slicing up about half the length of each), rub a bit of salt and ½ teaspoon of the turmeric among the eggplants into the cuts and leave for 20–30 minutes.

Heat 2 tablespoons of the oil in a medium saucepan over medium heat, add the panch phoran masala, onion and curry leaves and cook until the onion is golden brown. Add the ginger and garlic and cook for 1 minute. Add 2 tablespoons of water and the coriander, chilli powder and remaining turmeric and cook for 2 minutes. Add the tamarind pulp, masala paste and 1 litre (35 fl oz/4 cups) of water and cook for 20 minutes over low heat.

Meanwhile, heat the remaining oil in a frying pan over medium–high heat, add the eggplant and fry until lightly golden and sealed on all sides.

Once the sauce is cooked, add the eggplants and cook for about 10 minutes or until the eggplants are soft. Season with salt, add the capsicum and cook for 5 minutes — the capsicum does not need to be cooked for too long. Garnish with the curry leaves and ginger to serve.

Tip: To get a smooth paste while grinding, do not add too much water at one go. To increase the heat and sharpness, slit a green chilli and throw it in the mix towards the end with some curry leaves.

pakodi kadi

fried dumplings with yoghurt sauce

A summery Sunday afternoon lunch with the family is the perfect occasion for kadi to be made. All regions of India have a version of kadi, which is usually made from yoghurt when it starts to go sour. The Gujaratis add some sugar to it, while Southern Indians will add ground coconut, but regardless of the region, the one essential ingredient in a kadi is asafoetida. It can be made lighter if the fried dumplings are omitted. The perfect accompaniments are white rice, pappadoms and mango pickle. This is a favourite of my restaurant staff and of mine, especially when my young chef Dhanasekaran cooks it.

PAKODI

1 small onion, chopped

120 g (4¼ oz/1 cup) chickpea flour (besan)

⅛ teaspoon carom seeds (ajwain) (see glossary)

⅛ teaspoon bicarbonate of soda (baking soda)

2 tablespoons fine rice flour

1 teaspoon finely chopped coriander (cilantro)

¼ teaspoon finely grated ginger

¼ teaspoon red chilli powder

⅛ teaspoon ground turmeric

¼ teaspoon coriander seeds, crushed

vegetable or sunflower oil, for deep-frying

KADI

500 g (1 lb 2 oz/scant 2 cups) plain thick yoghurt

2 tablespoons vegetable or sunflower oil

40 g (1½ oz/⅓ cup) chickpea flour (besan)

2 teaspoons finely grated ginger

½ bunch coriander (cilantro), stalks only, finely chopped

1½ teaspoons red chilli powder

1 teaspoon ground turmeric

⅛ teaspoon asafoetida (see glossary)

TEMPERING

2 tablespoons vegetable or sunflower oil

¼ teaspoon black mustard seeds

1 dried red chilli

1 teaspoon coriander seeds

1 teaspoon cumin seeds

⅛ teaspoon asafoetida (see glossary)

1 sprig of curry leaves, leaves picked (optional)

To make the pakodi, combine all of the ingredients, except the oil, with 125 ml (4 fl oz/½ cup) of water, season with salt and set aside for 10 minutes.

Fill a wok or heavy-based saucepan one-third full with oil and heat to 170°C (338°F) or until a cube of bread turns golden brown in 20 seconds.

To make the pakodi, wet your fingers with oil or water as the mixture is quite sticky, then take small amounts (about a level dessertspoon) and form into small dumplings. Carefully drop into the oil as you make them. Deep-fry the pakodi for about 3–4 minutes or until golden brown but not crisp. Remove with a slotted spoon and drain on paper towel. You should have about 18 pakodi. Set aside.

To make the kadi, put all of the ingredients in a medium saucepan over medium heat and cook for 20 minutes, stirring very regularly so the yoghurt does not separate.

Add the fried pakodi, stirring to coat in the sauce, and cook for 5 minutes. Remove from the heat.

To make the tempering, heat the oil in a small frying pan over medium–high heat, add the mustard seeds and let them crackle for about 20 seconds. Add the remaining ingredients, except the curry leaves, and cook for 1 minute, then add the curry leaves. Pour this hot tempering carefully (as it may splash) into the kadi just prior to serving.

Serve hot.

chicken cafreal

green chicken curry

Each region of India makes a green chicken curry, and everyone has their own trick to 'green it up'. This cafreal is a Portuguese-influenced curry from Goa, which uses rum, a typical addition in Goan cooking, along with wine, but no other region of India uses alcohol in their cooking. The distinctive use of dark rum and coriander makes the finished colour of this dish a dark bottle green.

2 teaspoons ground turmeric

1 tablespoon finely grated ginger

2 teaspoons crushed garlic

1 tablespoon malt vinegar

1 kg (2 lb 4 oz) skinless, boneless chicken thigh fillets, each cut into 3

80 ml (2½ fl oz/⅓ cup) vegetable or sunflower oil

chilli oil, to garnish (optional)

GREEN MASALA PASTE

1 bunch coriander (cilantro), leaves picked

½ bunch mint, leaves picked

1 onion, chopped

4 small green chillies

5 cm (2 inch) piece of ginger

1 tablespoon white sugar

6 garlic cloves

5 cm (2 inch) piece of cinnamon stick

12 black peppercorns

6 whole cloves

2 teaspoons cumin seeds

3 tablespoons dark rum

2 tablespoons malt vinegar

Combine the turmeric, ginger, garlic, vinegar and ½ teaspoon of salt in a bowl, rub all over the chicken and leave to marinate in the fridge for 1 hour.

To make the green masala paste, put all of the ingredients in a blender or spice grinder and process to a fine paste. Heat the oil in a large heavy-based frying pan over medium–high heat, add the chicken and cook until golden brown on all sides.

Add the green masala paste and cook, covered, over low heat for 15–20 minutes or until the chicken is cooked through, removing the lid for the final 3 minutes of cooking to reduce the sauce slightly, if necessary. Drizzle with the chilli oil to serve.

paneer matar bhurji

cheese & peas curry

I discovered this dish at a small eatery called Kailash Parbat on Colaba Causeway in Mumbai (Bombay). It became my regular dining place on my days off from the Taj Mahal Palace Hotel. It was quite popular among the hotel staff at that time. That eatery continues to this day and you can still spot the odd chef from the Taj, enjoying his vegetarian meal.

3 tablespoons ghee (see glossary), melted

½ teaspoon cumin seeds

3 small green chillies, chopped

1 onion, finely chopped

1 tablespoon finely grated ginger

¼ teaspoon ground turmeric

1 teaspoon ground coriander

½ teaspoon dried fenugreek leaves (see glossary)

1 tomato, finely diced

300 g (10½ oz) paneer (curd cheese) (see glossary), crumbled, or cottage cheese

100 g (3½ oz/⅔ cup) green peas

3 tablespoons thin (pouring) cream

3 coriander (cilantro) sprigs, leaves picked

rotis (see glossary) or chapatis (see page 218), to serve

SERVES 4 AS PART OF A SHARED MEAL

Heat the ghee in a heavy-based saucepan over medium heat, add the cumin seeds and fry for 1 minute until brown. Add the chilli and cook for 1 minute. Add the onion and cook for 6–8 minutes or until brown. Add the ginger, turmeric, ground coriander, fenugreek leaves and tomato and cook for 5 minutes.

Add the paneer and peas and cook, covered for 5–7 minutes. Stir through the cream, season with salt and remove from the heat.

Garnish with the coriander leaves and serve hot. Serve with rotis or chapatis.

beef jardaloo

beef with apricots

This is a classic festive Parsi dish that I picked up during my time in Mumbai (Bombay). Parsi cooking has a heavy Persian influence, hence the use of dried fruit. This sweet, tangy and spicy dish is best enjoyed with either chapatis or a pilau.

200 g (7 oz/1¼ oz cups) dried apricots

4 cinnamon sticks

6 green cardamom pods

4 whole cloves

5 dried red chillies

2 teaspoons cumin seeds

2 teaspoons coriander seeds

30 ml (1 fl oz) malt vinegar

2 tablespoons sunflower oil

2 onions, chopped

½ teaspoon garam masala

2 tomatoes, chopped

600 g (1 lb 5 oz) beef rump steak, cubed

½ bunch coriander (cilantro), leaves roughly chopped

SERVES 4 AS PART OF A SHARED MEAL

Soak the apricots in 250 ml (9 fl oz/1 cup) of water, preferably overnight. Otherwise, soak in warm water for about 3 hours or until soft and swollen. Drain and set aside.

Put 2 of the cinnamon sticks in a spice grinder with the cardamom pods, cloves, dried chillies, and cumin and coriander seeds and grind to a fine powder. Add the vinegar and 1 tablespoon of water and blend to a paste. Set aside.

Heat the oil in a saucepan over medium heat, add the remaining cinnamon sticks and the onion and cook for 6–8 minutes or until the onion is brown.

Add the garam masala and the spice paste and cook, sprinkling over a little water so the spices don't burn, for 1–2 minutes or until you see the oil separating on the sides.

Add the tomato and cook for 2–3 minutes.

Add the beef and apricots and gently cook, covered, for about 30–40 minutes or until the beef is tender. Season with salt and garnish with the chopped coriander.

chatpata machli

tangy seared fish

½ teaspoon ground turmeric

1 tablespoon red chilli powder, plus extra for dusting

1 teaspoon ground black pepper

1 tablespoon coconut oil

1 teaspoon black mustard seeds

½ teaspoon fenugreek seeds

6 French shallots (eschalots), chopped

3 garlic cloves, sliced

150 ml (5 fl oz) tamarind water (see glossary)

200 ml (7 fl oz) coconut milk

800 g (1 lb 12 oz) snapper fillets

1 orange sweet potato

vegetable or sunflower oil, for deep-frying

1 tablespoon chopped coriander (cilantro)

Combine the turmeric, chilli powder and pepper with about 1 tablespoon of water to make a smooth paste.

Heat the coconut oil in a heavy-based saucepan over medium heat, add the mustard seeds and fenugreek seeds and let them crackle for about 20 seconds. Add the shallot and garlic and cook for 1 minute. Add the turmeric paste and cook for 2 minutes.

Stir in the tamarind water, season with salt and cook over low heat for 10 minutes.

Add the coconut milk and simmer for 2–3 minutes or until you have a thick paste. Remove from the heat and cool to room temperature.

Once cool, reserve 3 tablespoons of the mixture. Spread the remaining mixture all over the fish and put in the fridge to marinate for at least 2 hours.

While the fish is marinating, prepare the garnish. Peel and cut the sweet potato into matchstick-sized pieces. Fill a wok or heavy-based saucepan one-third full with oil and heat to 180°C (356°F) or until a cube of bread turns golden brown in 15 seconds. Fry the sweet potato matchsticks until crisp. Remove with a slotted spoon and drain on paper towel, then dust lightly with salt and chilli powder.

Heat the reserved coconut milk mixture with 2 tablespoons of water to make a sauce to drizzle over the fish.

Preheat a barbecue grill plate or chargrill pan to medium–high. Cook the fish for about 2 minutes each side or until cooked through.

Serve the fish with a little of the sauce drizzled over and garnished with the sweet potato matchsticks and coriander.

goan fish curry

1 kg (2 lb 4 oz) whole barramundi (or other firm white-fleshed fish), skin on, cut into finger-sized pieces, about 2 cm (¾ inch) wide

½ teaspoon ground turmeric

5 pieces of kokam (see glossary) or extra 1 tablespoon of tamarind pulp

1 long red chilli

3 tablespoons vegetable or sunflower oil

1 onion, sliced

1 teaspoon finely grated ginger

½ teaspoon crushed garlic

1 tablespoon tamarind pulp (see glossary)

50 ml (1½ fl oz) coconut cream

2 teaspoons finely shredded ginger, to garnish

MASALA PASTE

140 g (5 oz/1 cup) grated coconut (see glossary) or 150 g (5½ oz/ 1⅔ cups) desiccated coconut

8 Kashmiri dried red chillies (see glossary) or 1½ tablespoons sweet paprika

1 tablespoon coriander seeds

2 teaspoons cumin seeds

1 teaspoon black peppercorns

1 teaspoon ground turmeric

SERVES 6 AS PART OF A SHARED MEAL

Rub the fish with the turmeric and set aside for about 30 minutes. Soak the kokam in 250 ml (9 fl oz/1 cup) of hot water for about 10 minutes.

Prepare a chilli flower for garnish. Cut a cross in the bottom half of the red chilli and leave it in icy cold water for 5 minutes.

To make the masala paste, put all of the ingredients in a spice grinder and grind to a fine paste. Add 125 ml (4 fl oz/½ cup) of water and process into a smooth, fine paste.

Heat the oil in a large heavy-based saucepan over medium heat, add the onion and cook for 5 minutes. Add the ginger and garlic and cook for 2 minutes.

Add the masala paste and cook for 2 minutes.

Add the kokam and its soaking water and the tamarind pulp and simmer for 15 minutes over low heat.

Add the coconut cream and fish and cook for 5 minutes or until the fish is cooked. Garnish with the chilli flower and shredded ginger.

Tip: To get some extra flavour, marinate the fish with salt and chilli powder along with the ground turmeric.

crispy pork with ginger tamarind glaze

This dish appeared on the very first Abhi's menu. It was a special request from my dear friend, Tava. It has since become a favourite dish for quite a few of our regulars. It also makes a nice starter without the glaze.

RUB

1½ tablespoons coriander seeds, crushed

1½ tablespoons finely grated ginger

2 teaspoons cracked black pepper

2 teaspoons crushed garlic

1 teaspoon fennel seeds

½ teaspoon ground turmeric

1 teaspoon red chilli powder

1 teaspoon garam masala

juice of 1 lime

650 g (1 lb 7 oz) boneless pork belly, sliced

40 g (1½ oz/⅓ cup) chickpea flour (besan)

3 tablespoons cornflour (cornstarch)

vegetable or sunflower oil, for shallow-frying

5 cm (2 inch) piece of ginger, finely shredded

1 long red chilli, finely shredded

1 small green chilli, finely shredded

GINGER TAMARIND GLAZE

1 tablespoon vegetable oil

½ teaspoon black mustard seeds

2 teaspoons finely grated ginger

2 tablespoons tamarind pulp

2 tablespoons grated palm sugar (jaggery) or soft brown sugar

Combine all of the rub ingredients and season with salt. Rub all over the pork and set aside for 20 minutes.

Combine the chickpea flour and cornflour and season lightly with salt.

Heat the oil in a large frying pan over medium heat, dust the pork in the flour mixture, shaking off the excess, add to the pan and shallow-fry for about 6 minutes, turning regularly until crisp. Drain on a paper towel, then cut into finger-sized strips. Set aside.

To make the ginger tamarind glaze, heat the oil in a saucepan over medium–high heat, add the mustard seeds and let them crackle for 20 seconds. Add the ginger, tamarind, sugar and 3 tablespoons of water, bring to the boil and reduce until the sauce is a coating consistency.

Add the fried pork strips to the glaze and toss to coat. Garnish with the ginger and chilli.

patrani machi

fish steamed in banana leaves

800 g (1 lb 12 oz) blue-eye trevalla
fillets, cut into 4–6 portions

1 teaspoon ground turmeric

2–3 banana leaves

1 bunch coriander (cilantro),
roughly chopped

½ bunch mint, roughly chopped

2 small green chillies,
roughly chopped

5 cm (2 inch) piece of ginger,
roughly chopped

90 g (3¼ oz/1 cup) desiccated
coconut

2 teaspoons store-bought mango
chutney

½ teaspoon cumin seeds

juice of 1–2 limes

6–8 black peppercorns

lime wedges, to serve

Rub the fish with the turmeric and set aside to marinate for
15–20 minutes.

Cut the banana leaves into 4–6 squares large enough to enclose
a portion of fish. Line a large bamboo or metal steamer basket
with baking paper to prevent sticking.

Put the remaining ingredients, except the lime wedges, in a
small blender with ½ teaspoon of salt and process to a coarse paste.
Do not grind too finely or you will lose the texture of the coconut.

Put a portion of fish into the centre of each banana leaf and
apply a thick layer of the paste on top of the fish. Fold the sides
of the banana leaf over the fish to completely enclose and put,
fold side down, into the steamer basket. Cover with a tight-fitting
lid and steam over a saucepan or wok of simmering water for
10–15 minutes or until the fish is cooked through. Serve
immediately in the leaves with the lime wedges.

akoori

curried scrambled eggs

This is my typical start to the day. I can skip lunch or skip dinner but I can't skip akoori! My sons have been trained to make a perfect akoori as well. Much more than curried scrambled eggs, it has flavours that will give you a lift for the whole day. It is as light and energising as one can ever imagine. Akoori is a traditional Parsi dish and the trick is to keep the eggs soft and fluffy.

6–8 eggs, lightly beaten

1 tablespoon melted butter

2 tablespoons thin (pouring) cream

4–5 coriander (cilantro) sprigs, leaves chopped, plus extra to garnish

1 tablespoon vegetable or sunflower oil

1 teaspoon cumin seeds

2 French shallots (eschalots), finely chopped

2 small green chillies, seeds removed and finely chopped

2 teaspoons finely chopped ginger

1 teaspoon finely chopped garlic

¼ teaspoon ground turmeric, plus extra to garnish

1 tomato, finely chopped

toast, to serve

SERVES 4 FOR BREAKFAST

Put the eggs, butter, cream and coriander in a bowl, season with salt and combine.

Heat the oil in a large frying pan over medium heat, add the cumin seeds and allow them to sizzle for 1 minute.

Add the shallot and when almost brown, add the chilli, ginger and garlic and cook for 1 minute.

Add the turmeric, tomato and beaten egg mixture and cook over low heat, stirring constantly, until the eggs are cooked to the desired consistency. Check the seasoning and add salt if necessary.

Serve with toast and garnish the plate with the extra coriander and turmeric.

Tip: Remember the eggs will continue to cook even after you take them from the heat, so it is advisable to remove them a little underdone.

urulai chemeen charu

keralan prawn curry

This is a very light and simple recipe, greatly enjoyed by the Indian cricket team when they were in Sydney. Chef Biji at Abhi's excels at making this dish as it is his hometown recipe.

3 tablespoons vegetable
or sunflower oil

1 teaspoon black mustard seeds

10 French shallots (eschalots),
chopped

1 tablespoon finely grated ginger

2 teaspoons crushed garlic

5 new (baby) potatoes, quartered

4 small green chillies, chopped

2 tomatoes, chopped

70 g (2½ oz/½ cup) grated coconut
(see glossary) or 45 g (1½ oz/
½ cup) desiccated coconut

2 tablespoons tamarind pulp
(see glossary)

12 curry leaves

1 teaspoon red chilli powder

½ teaspoon ground turmeric

500 g (1 lb 2 oz) raw prawns
(shrimp), peeled with tails left
intact and deveined

SERVES 4 AS PART OF A SHARED MEAL

Heat the oil in a saucepan over medium heat, add the mustard seeds and let them crackle for about 20 seconds. Add the shallot and cook for about 5 minutes or until softened but not browned. Add the ginger and garlic and 1 tablespoon of water and cook for 1 minute.

Add the remaining ingredients, except the prawns, and cook, covered, over low heat or until the potato is almost cooked. Add the prawns and cook for 2–3 minutes or until cooked through.

meen pulli kozhambu

tamil fish curry

This is a simple dish of clean flavours. It is a unique Indian dish that does not use any ginger or garlic. The sauce can be made a day before use and kept in the fridge, and the fish curry will always taste better the next day. If available, a terracotta or baked clay pot is the best vessel to cook this fish curry in.

1 kg (2 lb 4 oz) skinless barramundi fillets

½ teaspoon ground turmeric

1 tablespoon Kashmiri chilli powder (see glossary)

3 tablespoons vegetable or sunflower oil

1 teaspoon black mustard seeds

2 dried red chillies

¼ teaspoon fenugreek seeds

½ teaspoon cumin seeds

1 large onion, sliced

1 teaspoon red chilli powder

2 teaspoons ground coriander

1 teaspoon ground cumin

125 ml (4 fl oz/½ cup) tamarind water (see glossary)

250 g (9 oz/1 cup) tomato paste (concentrated purée)

200 ml (7 fl oz) coconut milk

2 teaspoons white sugar (optional)

2 sprigs of curry leaves, leaves picked

SERVES 6 AS PART OF A SHARED MEAL

Rub the fish with the turmeric and half of the Kashmiri chilli powder and set aside to marinate for 20 minutes.

Heat the oil in a heavy-based saucepan over medium heat, add the mustard seeds and let them crackle for about 20 seconds. Add the dried chillies, fenugreek and cumin and cook for 1 minute or until fragrant and the tips of the chillies are blackened.

Add the onion and cook over low heat for 6–8 minutes or until the onion is softened but not browned.

Add the red chilli powder, remaining Kashmiri chilli powder, the coriander, cumin, tamarind, tomato paste and 250 ml (9 fl oz/1 cup) of water and cook, covered, over low heat for about 15 minutes.

Add the coconut milk and cook for 5 minutes. Taste and, if the tamarind is too sour, add the sugar to balance.

Add the fish and cook for 5 minutes or until the fish is cooked. Season with salt and serve garnished with the curry leaves.

madras prawn vendaki

prawn & okra curry

100 g (3½ oz/¾ cup) grated coconut (see glossary)

1 tablespoon roasted chana dal (see glossary)

80 ml (2½ fl oz/⅓ cup) gingili (unscented sesame oil) (see glossary)

2 teaspoons black or brown mustard seeds

1 teaspoon fenugreek seeds

1 tablespoon cumin seeds

100 g (3½ oz) French shallots (eschalots), sliced

100 g (3½ oz) okra, trimmed and cut a 3 cm (1¼ inch) slit on 1 side

1 tablespoon red chilli powder

2 tablespoons ground coriander

1 teaspoon ground turmeric

75 ml (2¼ fl oz) tamarind concentrate (see glossary)

2 tomatoes, diced

12 curry leaves

12 raw king prawns (shrimp), unpeeled

TEMPERING

1 tablespoon gingili (unscented sesame oil) (see glossary)

4 dried red chillies

8–10 curry leaves

SERVES 4–6 AS PART OF A SHARED MEAL

Put the coconut and chana dal in a spice grinder and finely grind. Ensure it is very finely ground — process in batches if necessary.

Heat the gingili in a large heavy-based saucepan over medium heat, add the mustard seeds and let them crackle for about 20 seconds. Add the fenugreek, cumin and shallot and cook for 2 minutes. Add the okra and cook for 5 minutes. Remove the okra mixture and set aside.

Add the chilli powder, coriander, turmeric, tamarind, tomato, coconut mixture and 750 ml (26 fl oz/3 cups) of water to the pan and cook for 5 minutes. Add half of the curry leaves, return the okra mixture to the pan and cook for 5 minutes.

Meanwhile, to make the tempering, heat the gingili in a small frying pan over low heat, add the chillies and curry leaves and cook for 1 minute or until fragrant. Remove from the heat.

Once the okra mixture is ready, add the prawns and cook for 2–3 minutes or until cooked through. Pour the tempering over the dish and serve immediately.

murghi nu farcha

parsi fried chicken

No Parsi wedding is complete without this dish. It is basically a spice-cooked chicken that is then egg-washed and fried. The eggs give a nice lacy texture to the dish.

¾ teaspoon ground turmeric

1 teaspoon red chilli powder

½ teaspoon ground cumin

6 skinless, boneless chicken thigh fillets, halved

80 ml (2½ fl oz/⅓ cup) vegetable or sunflower oil

1 small onion, chopped

2 small green chillies, sliced

2 teaspoons finely grated ginger

2 teaspoons crushed garlic

1 tomato, chopped

12 mint leaves, chopped

½ bunch coriander (cilantro), leaves roughly chopped

2 eggs

1 teaspoon garam masala

50 g (1¾ oz/⅓ cup) plain (all-purpose) flour

Combine ½ teaspoon of the turmeric with the chilli powder and cumin. Rub all over the chicken and leave to marinate in the fridge for 20 minutes.

Preheat the oven to 180°C (350°F/Gas 4).

Heat 2 tablespoons of the oil in a large ovenproof frying pan, add the onion and green chilli and cook for about 5 minutes or until the onion is brown. Add the ginger and garlic and cook, stirring regularly, for 2–3 minutes. Add the tomato and cook to a thick paste. Add the chicken and cook for 5 minutes or until the masala coats the chicken well.

Put the pan in the oven and roast for 5 minutes.

Remove from the oven, add the mint and half of the coriander, stir to mix well and set aside to cool.

Beat the eggs in a bowl, season with a little bit of salt and add the remaining coriander and turmeric and the garam masala.

Scrape off any excess sauce from the chicken, then dust in the flour.

Heat the remaining oil in a clean frying pan over medium–high heat. Dip the chicken in the egg mixture, allowing any excess to drip off, add the chicken to the pan and cook until golden brown all over. Drain on paper towel and serve immediately.

dhaba aloo murg

chicken & potato curry

A dhaba is an inexpensive eatery, often frequented by travellers for a roadside meal. It's essentially an Indian truck stop. This particular chicken and potato dish was one of our favourites on our travels — we enjoyed it in Delhi on our way to Agra. Luckily we had the luxury of a driver after such a fulfilling meal!

1.4 kg (3 lb 2 oz) skinless chicken thigh fillets (see tip)

300 g (10½ oz) plain thick yoghurt, beaten

80 g (2¾ oz/⅓ cup) ghee (see glossary)

2 tablespoons vegetable or sunflower oil

6 green cardamom pods

2 cinnamon sticks

4 red onions, sliced

1 tablespoon finely grated ginger

2 teaspoons crushed garlic

90 g (3¼ oz/⅓ cup) tomato paste (concentrated purée)

2 teaspoons red chilli powder

3 teaspoons ground coriander

½ teaspoon garam masala

4–6 small new (baby) potatoes, skin on, halved

6 coriander (cilantro) sprigs, leaves roughly chopped

SERVES 6 AS PART OF A SHARED MEAL

Coat the chicken with the yoghurt and leave to marinate for 30 minutes in the fridge to allow the yoghurt to tenderise the chicken.

Put the ghee and oil in a large heavy-based saucepan over medium heat, add the cardamom and cinnamon and cook for about 1 minute or until fragrant. Add the onion and cook for 8–10 minutes or until golden brown. Add the ginger and garlic and fry for 2 minutes. Add the tomato paste, chilli powder, ground coriander and garam masala, season with salt, drizzle over 1–2 tablespoons of water and cook for 7–10 minutes or until the oil separates, scraping the base of the pan regularly.

Add the chicken and cook, covered, for 10–15 minutes or until the chicken is tender (see tip). Add the potato and 250 ml (9 fl oz/ 1 cup) of water and cook for about 30 minutes or until the potato is tender. Season with salt and garnish with the coriander.

Tip: This tastes better if made with free-range skinless chicken on the bone. The chicken takes slightly longer to cook but the pay-off is in the great flavour.

If you prefer this dish hotter, fry four green chillies in vegetable oil and add during finishing.

lagan nu cushter

parsi wedding custard

My dear friend and mentor chef Cyrus Todiwala of Café Spice Namasté in London shares this recipe. I first tasted lagan nu cushter when I joined the Taj Mahal Palace Hotel, Bombay in 1977 and chef Cyrus was in charge of the kitchen. This custard was not the only sweet surprise waiting for me. At the Taj I had found a mentor in chef Cyrus, who was to become the major influence in my cooking career.

750 ml (26 fl oz/3 cups) milk

600 ml (21 fl oz) thin (pouring) cream

110 g (3¾ oz/½ cup) white sugar

3 eggs (free-range and organic is preferable)

½ teaspoon ground green cardamom

½ teaspoon grated nutmeg

1 tablespoon rosewater

1 vanilla bean, halved lengthways

2 teaspoons charoli (chironji) (see glossary)

3 pistachio nuts, thinly sliced

2 raw almonds, sliced

butter, to grease

SERVES 8 AS A DESSERT

Preheat the oven to 140°C (275°F/Gas 1).

Put the milk and 400 ml (14 fl oz) of the cream in a casserole dish or heavy-based saucepan and bring to the boil, remembering that milk overflows very quickly and also burns at the base very rapidly. As soon as it comes to the boil, reduce the heat to a simmer and cook until reduced by roughly half, the colour is a lovely pale brown and it is slightly caramelised. When simmering, one way to avoid losing valuable skin is to constantly brush down the sides of the pan using a wet pastry brush. As the skin forms on the surface, skim it off, reserving for later use.

Once reduced by half, add the sugar and simmer, stirring constantly for 3–5 minutes. Remove from the heat and allow to cool slightly. When it is a bit cooler but still quite warm, put the milk and the collected skin in a blender and blend until smooth.

Put the eggs, remaining cream, the cardamom, nutmeg and rosewater in a large bowl and scrape in the seeds from the vanilla bean. Blend with a hand-held stick blender to combine. Gradually pour the warm milk into the egg mixture, whisking constantly.

Pour the mixture into eight greased 150 ml (5 fl oz) capacity ramekins or a greased 1.5 litre (52 fl oz) capacity baking dish and sprinkle the nuts over evenly. Sit the ramekins or dish in a roasting tray and fill with water to almost half the height of the dish or ramekins. Bake for about 40 minutes. To check the custard is cooked, insert a thin small knife in the centre; if it comes out clean, the custard is set. Ideally you should also get a nice colour on top. Remove from the oven and water bath. Cool to room temperature before serving, or chill to serve.

бебіпса

goan layer cake

*I tasted this classic Goan dessert for the first time when Abhi's first head chef, Amitava Guha,
put it on our menu. It is extremely time consuming to make but the method is simple
and the result well worth it.*

300 g (10½ oz/2 cups) plain (all-purpose) flour

½ teaspoon grated nutmeg

440 ml (15½ fl oz) coconut milk

240 g (8½ oz) white sugar

4 egg yolks

10 green cardamom pods, crushed

2 vanilla beans, halved lengthways

125 g (4½ oz/½ cup) ghee (see glossary), melted

vanilla bean ice cream and/or crème anglaise, to serve (optional)

SERVES 6–8 AS A DESSERT

Sift the flour and nutmeg together and set aside. Put the coconut milk, sugar, egg yolks and cardamom pods in a large bowl and scrape the seeds from the vanilla beans into the bowl. Gently blend using a hand-held stick blender until combined. Strain through a fine sieve into a large bowl.

Fold in the flour mixture to make a smooth batter similar to a pancake batter, adding 2–3 tablespoons of water if the batter seems too thick. The consistency of the batter is the key. Set aside to rest for 45 minutes.

Preheat the oven to 180°C (350°F/Gas 4).

Lightly grease a 20 cm (8 inch) round or square cake tin with the melted ghee and pour in one ladle of batter, just enough to form a 1 cm (½ inch) thick layer, swirling to coat the base of the tin. Bake for 15 minutes or until the top is dark brown. The top part of the layer needs to caramelise before adding the next layer.

Apply some more ghee to the cooked layer before adding the next ladle of batter and bake again. Repeat until you run out of batter (you should end up with about 8 layers). The trick is to get multiple layers but still maintain a cake-like consistency (see tip).

Once the cake is complete, cool and remove from the tin. Slice into triangles and serve warm or cold either with vanilla ice cream and/or crème anglaise.

Tip: You can also cook this under a grill (broiler).

Do not be alarmed if you overbrown a layer, just keep adding the batter, layer by layer. The latter layers will require less cooking time than the first ones.

spice

MARRIAGE IS THE SPICE OF LIFE. Spice brings out the flavour in any dish and is an integral and indispensable part of Indian cuisine. It adds excitement, colour and life.

On 12 July 1987, my destiny and Suba's became entwined. Our marriage was arranged by our families in consultation with an astrologer, so it was already written in the stars for Suba to become an indispensable part of my life — the must-add spice in all my endeavours.

When Indians talk of spice, they're referring to aromatic flavours and not heat. Chilli is not a spice. The world of Indian spices is as colourful and varied as the continent itself. It's all about the intricate and delicate use of the right spice for a dish. Masala is a general term for a spice mix and it is the cornerstone of Indian cooking, forming the basis for any good curry. A masala might consist of only two spices or twenty. One of the best known is garam masala (garam means warm) and every region has its own particular version using differing combinations. And, of course, all good cooks have their very own secret recipe.

Spices are India's gift to the world. India grows more than fifty different spices and produces 2.7 million tonnes annually, accounting for about half the world's spice production. Sangli, in Maharashtra, where Suba once lived and studied, is known as Turmeric City because it has Asia's biggest turmeric-selling market. Pepper, sometimes known as black gold, is the most important traded spice in the world and the name comes from the Tamil word pippali.

The important thing about using spices is ensuring they're fresh. Whole spices keep longer than ground, which you should try to use within twelve months. Always keep them in airtight containers, rather than ripped-open bags, and away from heat and light.

When I was growing up, my grandmother Meenakshi never used fennel seeds in her cooking. Priests and Brahmins had less spices in their cooking, believing it aroused the senses, including lust, but my grandmother loved cloves, cardamom, cinnamon, nutmeg and pepper. These spices created a lighter, simpler flavour to our family's food that influences my cooking to this day.

While I use fennel, I avoid creating complex masalas using thirty-six different spices, believing that it's better to taste the individual flavours of spices and the way they affect the food.

If you're not used to using spices, you may be nervous at first but the instant you taste the dish you will wonder how you have lived your life without them, they are what's been missing without you realising it … this was how I felt when I met my spice girl, Suba.

chicken chukka

chettiyar chicken

This Southern Indian dish packs a punch in flavour, with its robust spicing. It originates from the region of Chettinad, in a city called Karaikudi. The affluent Chettiyars often travelled to Myanmar (Burma) and other countries for timber trade and thus brought a variety of spices back to India; naturally the use of spices in Chettiyar cuisine is abundant. Originally, spices were used in India partly to disguise and improve poor ingredients, but now I use them to enhance flavours.

**120 ml (4 fl oz) vegetable
or sunflower oil**

2 red onions, sliced

1 tablespoon crushed garlic

**5 cm (2 inch) piece of ginger, finely
shredded**

2 tomatoes, chopped

**8 skinless chicken pieces
(thigh, breast and leg)**

12 curry leaves

MASALA PASTE

2 tablespoons coriander seeds

100 g (3½ oz) desiccated coconut

1 tablespoon cumin seeds

1 tablespoon black peppercorns

2 teaspoons fennel seeds

10 dried red chillies

6 whole cloves

4 fresh bay leaves

**3 pieces of cassia bark
(or cinnamon)**

3 green cardamom pods

2 star anise

SERVES 4–6 AS PART OF A SHARED MEAL

To make the masala paste, heat a medium dry frying pan over medium heat, add the coriander seeds and lightly toast for about 1 minute, shaking the pan regularly. Add the remaining ingredients and cook for 2 minutes or until fragrant and slightly coloured, stirring regularly. This is done to release the flavours of the whole spices before grinding. Grind the spices in a spice grinder until finely ground. Add 60–125 ml (2–4 fl oz/¼–½ cup) of water and grind to a semi-smooth paste.

Heat 80 ml (2½ fl oz/⅓ cup) of the oil in a large heavy-based saucepan over medium heat, add the onion and cook for 6–8 minutes or until golden brown. Add the garlic and ginger (reserving some ginger to garnish) and cook for 1 minute. Stir in the tomato and cook for 2 minutes.

Add the masala paste and the chicken and stir gently to coat the chicken pieces.

Add 125 ml (4 fl oz/½ cup) of water and cook, covered, over low heat for 20 minutes or until the chicken is cooked.

While the chicken is cooking, heat the remaining oil in a frying pan over low heat and fry half of the curry leaves for 1–2 minutes or until just crisp. Set aside.

Once the chicken is cooked, add the remaining curry leaves and cook for 2 minutes. Remove from the heat and serve garnished with the ginger and fried curry leaves.

gutti venkai koora

stuffed eggplant

Gutti venkai koora literally translates to stuffed, eggplant, dry. Powerful, enigmatic spices, full of flavour and texture. This dish is loved by the staff (particularly our Andhra regiment!) at Abhi's.

12 baby eggplants (aubergines)

2 tablespoons tamarind pulp (see glossary)

125 ml (4 fl oz/½ cup) vegetable or sunflower oil

¼ teaspoon black mustard seeds

⅛ teaspoon fenugreek seeds

½ teaspoon split urad dal (black lentils/black gram) (see glossary)

10 curry leaves

2 dried red chillies

finely shredded ginger, to garnish

FILLING

1 tablespoon vegetable oil

2 onions, thinly sliced

6 garlic cloves, finely chopped

3 dried red chillies

3 tablespoons raw peanuts

3 tablespoons desiccated coconut

1 tablespoon coriander seeds

1 teaspoon cumin seeds

2 teaspoons chana dal (see glossary)

¼ teaspoon asafoetida (see glossary)

¼ teaspoon white sesame seeds

10 curry leaves

SERVES 4–5 AS PART OF A SHARED MEAL

Slit each eggplant from the base into quarters, but do not slit all the way, just enough to make a space to put the filling inside. Sprinkle a bit of salt onto the cut eggplant and set aside.

To make the filling, heat the oil in a frying pan over medium heat, add the onion and garlic and cook for 6–8 minutes or until light brown. Set aside to cool.

Heat a small dry frying pan over medium heat and lightly toast, one ingredient at a time, the chillies, peanuts, coconut, coriander seeds, cumin seeds, chana dal, asafoetida, sesame seeds and curry leaves. Toast each, shaking the pan regularly, until fragrant but not burnt. Add all of the toasted ingredients to the onion mixture.

Put the tamarind pulp in a small bowl. Add 250 ml (9 fl oz/ 1 cup) of water and combine. Set aside.

Fill the eggplant openings with the filling.

Heat 2 tablespoons of the oil in a large heavy-based frying pan over medium–high heat, add the eggplant and fry until lightly golden and sealed on all sides. Remove from the pan.

Heat the remaining oil in the same pan over medium–high heat, add the mustard seeds and let them crackle for 20–30 seconds. Add the fenugreek, urad dal, curry leaves and dried chillies and cook for 1 minute.

Put the filled eggplants carefully into the pan and cook, covered, for 7–8 minutes or until soft, shaking the pan occasionally. Be careful not to shake too hard as you will break the eggplants.

When the eggplants are soft to the touch, remove the lid, stir in the tamarind mixture and cook, uncovered, for 7–10 minutes or until the sauce has reduced to a coating consistency. Garnish with the ginger and serve.

palak patta chaat

indian street snack

This famous roadside favourite is traditionally not a dish prepared in Indian homes. It's a dish best eaten outside in the middle of a shopping spree. The regular dish comprises wheat crisps covered in yoghurt, and tamarind and coriander chutneys. I gave the dish a makeover at Abhi's with battered and fried spinach leaves replacing the humble wheat crisps. The tamarind chutney has the addition of sweet dates to balance its sourness.

FRIED SPINACH LEAVES

150 g (5½ oz/1¼ cups)
chickpea flour (besan)

50 g (1¾ oz) rice flour

½ teaspoon red chilli powder

2 teaspoons salt

peanut or canola oil,
for deep-frying

1 bunch English spinach,
leaves picked, washed and patted dry
(you will need about 20 leaves)

MINT & CORIANDER CHUTNEY

½ bunch mint, leaves picked

1 bunch coriander (cilantro),
roughly chopped

4 long green chillies, chopped

1 tablespoon lemon juice

2 teaspoons finely grated ginger

¼ teaspoon ground black pepper

1 teaspoon salt

DATE & TAMARIND CHUTNEY

30 g (1 oz) pitted dates, chopped

1 tablespoon tamarind concentrate
(see glossary)

1 tablespoon grated palm sugar (jaggery)

2½ teaspoons ground cumin

TOMATO CHILLI CHUTNEY

2 ripe tomatoes

4 long red chillies, chopped

2½ teaspoons sweet paprika

YOGHURT DRESSING

1 tablespoon ground cumin

260 g (9¼ oz/1 cup) Greek-style yoghurt

1 tablespoon caster (superfine) sugar

TO SERVE

100 g (3½ oz) sebago potato, boiled
until tender, peeled, then diced

125 g (4½ oz) tinned chickpeas,
rinsed and drained

2 teaspoons chopped coriander (cilantro)

To make the fried spinach leaves, first make the batter. Combine the flours, chilli powder and salt in a bowl. Make a well in the centre, then gradually add 290 ml (10 fl oz) of water and whisk until smooth. Cover and set aside until required.

To make the mint and coriander chutney, put all of the ingredients in a food processor and process until smooth. Transfer to a small bowl, cover and set aside until required.

To make the date and tamarind chutney, combine all of the ingredients in a small saucepan, add 80 ml (2½ fl oz/⅓ cup) of water and cook over low heat for 10 minutes or until the dates have softened. Strain through a fine mesh sieve into a bowl, discarding the solids. Cool, then cover and set aside until required.

To make the tomato chilli chutney, score a shallow cross in the base of the tomatoes. Put in a heatproof bowl and cover with boiling water. Leave for 30 seconds, then transfer to cold water and peel the skin away from the cross. Cut the tomatoes in half, scoop out the seeds with a teaspoon and discard. Roughly dice the flesh, combine with the chilli and paprika in a small saucepan over low heat

and simmer for 10–15 minutes or until soft. Strain the mixture through a fine mesh sieve, discarding the liquid. Cool, then cover and set aside until required.

To make the yoghurt dressing, heat a small frying pan over medium–high heat, add the cumin and dry-fry for about 30 seconds, shaking the pan regularly. Put the yoghurt and sugar in a bowl, add the cumin and stir to combine. Cover and refrigerate until required.

When you're ready to serve, fry the spinach leaves. To do this, heat about 10 cm (4 inches) of oil in a deep-fryer or large saucepan to 180°C (356°F) or until a cube of bread turns golden brown in 15 seconds. Dip the spinach leaves, one at a time, into the batter, shaking off any excess, and deep-fry, in batches, until crisp and golden. Remove with a slotted spoon and drain on paper towel.

To serve, divide the fried spinach leaves among plates, scatter with the potato and chickpeas, spoon over a little yoghurt dressing, then top with 1 teaspoon of each of the chutneys. Sprinkle with the coriander and serve immediately.

mysore kozhi

mysore chilli chicken

1 kg (2 lb 4 oz) boneless, skinless chicken thigh fillets, each cut into 3

130 g (4½ oz/½ cup) plain thick yoghurt

100 g (3½ oz) grated coconut (see glossary)

80 ml (2½ fl oz/⅓ cup) vegetable or sunflower oil

6 green cardamom pods

2 x 2.5 cm (1 inch) pieces of cinnamon stick

6 whole cloves

1 onion, sliced

1 tablespoon finely grated ginger

1 tablespoon crushed garlic

2 teaspoons ground turmeric

1 tablespoon Kashmiri chilli powder (see glossary)

1 tomato, chopped

4 small green chillies, halved lengthways

100 ml (3½ fl oz) coconut milk

finely shredded ginger and finely chopped coriander (cilantro), to garnish (optional)

Combine the chicken and yoghurt and leave to marinate for 20 minutes.

Put half of the coconut in a spice grinder with 125 ml (4 fl oz/½ cup) of water and blend to a fine paste — it's very important that it is a fine paste. Remove from the spice grinder and set aside. Repeat with the remaining coconut and another 125 ml (4 fl oz/½ cup) of water. Set aside.

Heat the oil in a heavy-based saucepan over medium heat, add the cardamom, cinnamon and cloves and cook for about 1 minute or until fragrant. Add the onion and cook for 6–8 minutes or until golden brown. Add the ginger and garlic and cook for 1 minute. Add the turmeric and chilli powder, tomato and green chilli and cook for 2 minutes.

Add the ground coconut paste with 250 ml (9 fl oz/1 cup) of water and cook, covered, for 15 minutes.

Add the chicken and cook, covered, for 15 minutes.

Stir in the coconut milk and cook for 5 minutes or until the chicken is cooked and tender. Garnish with the ginger and coriander to serve.

aki's railway goat curry

Our goat curry has survived the many menu changes over the years. In India, mutton refers to goat meat (not sheep as it does here). This dish is cooked on the bone to deliver succulent pieces of goat in a rich sauce. It was originally a travellers' meal on the Southern Indian railways. It's said that the dish was created when a train hit a goat on the tracks … Bingo, goat curry! We have modified it, replacing the more traditional coconut oil and added our unique spicing.

100 ml (3½ fl oz) sunflower oil

3 dried bay leaves

2.5 cm (1 inch) piece of cinnamon stick

6 green cardamom pods

9 whole cloves

2 red onions, thinly sliced

2 teaspoons crushed garlic

1½ tablespoons finely grated ginger

½ teaspoon ground turmeric

1 teaspoon red chilli powder

1 tablespoon ground coriander

3 tomatoes, chopped

1.5 kg (3 lb 5 oz) goat leg, bone in, cut into 2 cm (¾ inch) cubes (ask your butcher to do this)

4 coriander (cilantro) sprigs, plus whole leaves to garnish

pinch of mace threads or ground mace

SERVES 8–10 AS PART OF A SHARED MEAL

Heat the oil in a casserole dish over medium–low heat, add the bay leaves, cinnamon stick, cardamom and cloves and cook until fragrant. Add the onion and cook for 8–10 minutes or until golden brown. Add the garlic and cook for 1 minute. Add the ginger, turmeric, chilli powder and ground coriander and cook for 2 minutes, adding 1 tablespoon of water to stop the ground spices from burning.

Add the tomato and cook until you see some oil separation around the edges.

Add the goat, season with salt, stir to coat the meat with the mixture and continue to stir regularly for 5 minutes or until the meat releases its juices.

Add 1 litre (35 fl oz/4 cups) of water, bring to the boil, then cook, covered, for 1½ hours. Check the consistency of the sauce. It should not be too thin; if it is, cook, uncovered, for 20–30 minutes. Add the whole sprigs of coriander and the mace and remove from the heat. Garnish with the coriander leaves.

tip: Slow cooking will ensure tender meat.

masala lamb cutlets

You should ask my next-door butcher about this dish. He has been my meat supplier from day one for both restaurants. The secret to this dish is the quality of the lamb; his is from Junee in the Riverina region in New South Wales. When the meat is this good, it doesn't need much treatment.

1 teaspoon ground mace

1 teaspoon ground cardamom

2 teaspoons fennel seeds

2 cm (¾ inch) piece of ginger, roughly chopped

3 garlic cloves, bruised

½ bunch coriander (cilantro), leaves and stalks

3 tablespoons lime juice

1 teaspoon Kashmiri chilli powder (see glossary)

½ teaspoon ground turmeric

12 French-trimmed lamb cutlets

¼ teaspoon saffron threads

3 tablespoons plain thick yoghurt

1 tablespoon olive oil

SERVES 6 AS PART OF A SHARED MEAL

Combine the mace, cardamom and fennel in a bowl to make a garam masala and set aside.

Using a mortar and pestle or small spice grinder, grind the ginger, garlic and a pinch of salt to a paste. Add the coriander leaves and stalks and grind to a paste. Transfer to a large bowl.

Add the garam masala, lime juice, chilli powder, turmeric and ½ teaspoon of salt to the bowl and combine. Add the lamb and toss to coat well, then cover and marinate in the fridge for 2 hours.

Put the saffron threads in a small bowl with 30 ml (1 fl oz) of boiling water. Cool, then add the yoghurt, season with a little salt and stir until smooth. Add to the lamb and coat well.

Preheat the oven to 180°C (350°F/Gas 4) and line a baking tray with baking paper.

Heat the oil in a large frying pan pan over medium–high heat, add the lamb, in batches, and cook for 1 minute each side to seal. Transfer to the prepared tray and roast for 5–7 minutes for medium or until cooked to your liking. Rest for 4 minutes before serving.

kesar badami khurma

saffron chicken curry

A rich saffron chicken dish that balances nutty goodness with the tasty overtones of yoghurt and cream. It makes a proud and regular appearance in the cooking demonstrations I host at Abhi's. This is a dish for those who demand some curry inspiration. The simplicity of the dish is in the limited use of spice.

100 g (3½ oz) blanched almonds

50 g (1¾ oz/⅓ cup) cashew nuts

2 tablespoons ghee
(see glossary)

2 tablespoons vegetable
or sunflower oil

3–4 green cardamom pods

2–3 cinnamon sticks

1 teaspoon red chilli powder

1 tablespoon ground coriander

5 saffron threads

2 red onions, sliced

1 tablespoon finely grated ginger

1 tablespoon crushed garlic

150 g (5½ oz) plain thick
yoghurt, beaten

1 kg (2 lb 4 oz) chicken
thigh fillets, each cut into 3

100 ml (3½ fl oz) thin
(pouring) cream

6 coriander (cilantro) sprigs,
roughly chopped

SERVES 6 AS PART OF A SHARED MEAL

Soak the almonds and cashew nuts in a bowl of hot water for 1 hour, then drain. Put in a spice grinder (see glossary) and grind to a smooth paste — it's important to get it very smooth so you may need to do this a couple of times. Set aside.

Heat the ghee and oil in a large heavy-based saucepan over medium heat, add the cardamom, cinnamon, chilli powder, ground coriander and saffron and cook for 1 minute or until fragrant. Add the onion and cook until golden brown. Add the ginger and garlic and cook for 2 minutes.

Mix the beaten yoghurt with the nut paste, add to the pan and cook, semi-covered, over low heat for 10–15 minutes, gradually adding 500 ml (17 fl oz/2 cups) of water as necessary, to prevent the masala burning and catching on the base of the pan.

When the sauce is cooked and the oil begins to separate, add the chicken, season with salt and cook, covered, over medium heat for 15–20 minutes or until the chicken is cooked and tender. Stir in the cream and garnish with the chopped coriander.

Tip: The secret to making this dish is to allow the sauce to cook well over medium heat and to only add the chicken pieces when the sauce is nearly done.

lamb kozhambu

cashew nut & coconut lamb curry

How do you pronounce this one? Cooking it is easier than spelling it. It's a common South Indian household meal that doesn't involve laborious cooking.

60 g (2¼ oz/⅔ cup) desiccated coconut

3 tablespoons cashew nuts

1 tablespoon poppy seeds

80 ml (2½ fl oz/⅓ cup) vegetable or sunflower oil

1 teaspoon fennel seeds

3 green cardamom pods

5 whole cloves

1 cinnamon stick

1 large onion, thinly sliced

1 tablespoon finely grated ginger

1 tablespoon crushed garlic

1 teaspoon ground turmeric

2 teaspoons red chilli powder

1 tablespoon ground coriander

2 tomatoes, diced

500 g (1 lb 2 oz) boneless lamb leg, cut into 4 cm (1½ inch cubes)

500 g (1 lb 2 oz) boneless lamb shoulder, cut into 4 cm (1½ inch) cubes

1 teaspoon freshly ground black pepper

juice of 1 lime

1 bunch coriander (cilantro), leaves roughly chopped

SERVES 4–6 AS PART OF A SHARED MEAL

Soak the coconut, cashew nuts and poppy seeds in 170 ml (5½ fl oz/⅔ cup) of water for 20 minutes. Put in a spice grinder and grind to a smooth paste — you may need to do this in two batches. It is very important that the coconut and cashew nuts are fine and smooth, otherwise it will affect the finished dish.

Heat the oil in a large heavy-based saucepan over medium–high heat, add the fennel, cardamom, cloves and cinnamon and cook for 2 minutes or until fragrant and lightly coloured. Add the onion and cook for about 8 minutes or until brown. Add the ginger and garlic and cook for 2 minutes.

Combine the turmeric, chilli powder and ground coriander with 2 tablespoons of water to make a paste, then add to the pan and cook for 5 minutes, gradually adding 3 tablespoons of water until the oil separates.

Add the tomato and another 3 tablespoons of water and cook, covered, for 5 minutes or until the tomato breaks down.

Season with salt and add the lamb, cover, and cook until the lamb is sealed on all sides.

When the lamb releases its juices, add 750 ml (26 fl oz/3 cups) of water and cook, covered, over high heat for about 30 minutes.

Add the coconut paste and cook, covered, for 20 minutes or until the lamb is tender. Add the pepper.

Once the lamb is tender, add the lime juice and coriander leaves. Remove from the heat and rest for 5 minutes before serving.

goan pork sausage curry

I first encountered this curry many years ago at my friend Noel Rodriguez's house. He is from Goa, once a Portuguese colony, and the Goan sausage traditionally used in this dish is a relative of the Portuguese chorizo, only much spicier as it is has been adapted and made with the spices available in India. The potatoes act as an excellent foil to the heat of the chilli in the dish.

3 tablespoons vegetable or sunflower oil

½ teaspoon cumin seeds

1 large onion, sliced

1 tablespoon finely grated ginger

2 teaspoons crushed garlic

½ teaspoon ground turmeric

1 teaspoon ground cumin

1 teaspoon red chilli powder

2 teaspoons ground coriander

1 tomato, diced

1 tablespoon malt vinegar

4 new (baby) potatoes, skin on, cut into 2 cm (¾ inch) slices

600 g (1 lb 5 oz) spicy fresh pork sausage (such as chorizo), casings removed and meat cut into 2 cm (¾ inch) slices

finely chopped coriander (cilantro), to garnish

SERVES 4–6 AS PART OF A SHARED MEAL

Heat the oil in a heavy-based frying pan over medium heat, add the cumin seeds and cook for 1 minute.

Add the onion and cook over medium–low heat for about 5 minutes or until softened and translucent but do not brown.

Add the ginger and garlic and cook for 1 minute.

Add the turmeric, cumin, chilli powder, ground coriander and tomato and cook for 5–7 minutes, adding 1–2 tablespoons of water to prevent the spices sticking to the base of the pan.

Add 375 ml (13 fl oz/1½ cups) of water, the vinegar, potato and sausage and cook for 10–15 minutes or until the potato and sausage are cooked. Check the seasoning and garnish with the coriander to serve.

duck mappas

keralan duck curry

This is a very popular dish at Aki's. It's rich in flavour, light in consistency and sweet from the flavour of the coconut and French shallots. Not much additional oil is required to cook this dish as the duck breasts cook in their own fat. Duck is not the most popular meat in India but the Keralites relish this dish.

6 duck breasts with skin and wing bone (see tip)

2 teaspoons red chilli powder

2 teaspoons finely grated ginger

50 ml (1½ fl oz) coconut oil

4 green cardamom pods

6 whole cloves

1 cinnamon stick

2 long green chillies, thinly sliced diagonally

2 sprigs of curry leaves

12 French shallots (eschalots), chopped

5 cm (2 inch) piece of ginger, finely shredded

250 ml (9 fl oz/1 cup) coconut milk

80 ml (2½ fl oz/⅓ cup) coconut cream

appams or iddiappams (see page 184), to serve

SERVES 6 AS PART OF A SHARED MEAL

Preheat the oven to 160°C (315°F/Gas 2–3) and put a baking dish in the oven to heat up.

Score the duck skin a few times with a knife, then rub the skin and meat with the chilli powder, ginger and a little salt. Put in the fridge to marinate for 30 minutes.

Heat a large heavy-based frying pan over high heat, add 1 tablespoon of the coconut oil and cook the duck in two batches, skin side down, for about 3 minutes or until sealed. Turn over and seal the other side. This is just to seal the meat — do not overcook. Transfer the duck to the preheated baking dish and roast for 20 minutes. Remove the duck and set aside. Drain the excess fat from the baking dish but reserve the juices and set aside for adding to the sauce later.

Heat the remaining coconut oil in a large frying pan over medium–high heat. Add the cardamom, cloves, cinnamon, green chilli and curry leaves and let these splutter for a few seconds. Reduce the heat to low, add the shallot and cook for 5 minutes or until softened but without browning.

Add the ginger, coconut milk, reserved duck juices and 125 ml (4 fl oz/½ cup) of water. Add the duck breasts and cook, covered, over low heat for 15 minutes or until the duck is almost cooked.

Add the coconut cream and cook, uncovered, for 5 minutes. Remove the duck from the pan and thickly slice, then return to the sauce. Serve with appams or iddiappams.

Tip: If you can't find duck breasts with the wing bone attached, simply use duck breasts. Roasting the duck slowly at a low heat will keep them juicy and tender.

tandoori chooza

tandoori spatchcock

1 x 1 kg (2 lb 4 oz) spatchcock (baby chicken), butterflied

½ teaspoon ground turmeric

1 teaspoon red chilli powder

1 tablespoon finely grated ginger

2 teaspoons crushed garlic

3 tablespoons malt vinegar

3 tablespoons Greek-style yoghurt

3 tablespoons mustard oil (see glossary)

2 tablespoons melted butter or ghee (see glossary)

mint and yoghurt sauce (see page 212), to serve

GARAM MASALA

1 teaspoon grated nutmeg

1 teaspoon ground mace

½ teaspoon ground cardamom

½ teaspoon ground cloves

½ teaspoon ground star anise

2 teaspoons ground cumin

SERVES 2–3 AS PART OF A SHARED MEAL

Remove the skin from the spatchcock and score each breast. Combine the turmeric, chilli powder, ginger, garlic, vinegar and ½ teaspoon of salt in a bowl and rub over the spatchcock to coat well. Put in the fridge to marinate for at least 3 hours.

Combine all of the garam masala ingredients in a small bowl.

Put the yoghurt in a bowl and beat until smooth, then add the garam masala, a touch of salt and the mustard oil and stir to combine. Rub all over the spatchcock. Put in the fridge to marinate for another 3 hours.

Remove the spatchcock from the fridge 20 minutes before cooking to bring to room temperature.

Preheat a barbecue or grill (broiler) to hot. Thread two long metal skewers through the bird crossways to make it easier to handle. Cook on the barbecue with the breast facing the heat for 6 minutes or until cooked through, or under the grill for 10–12 minutes. Ensure both the thigh and breast meat is cooked by testing with a metal skewer — the juices should run clear with no traces of pink.

Remove the spatchcock and let it rest for 5 minutes. Cut into pieces, brush with the melted butter or ghee and serve with the mint and yoghurt sauce.

kundan kaliyan

golden lamb curry

The traditional version of this dish for the Nawabs incorporated edible gold leaves. Kundan means gold and kaliyan translates to meat strips. The Nawabs did not like chewing whole spices in their mouth hence it is cooked in two stages: the meat is first cooked with the whole spices, then the sauce is strained so the texture is smooth and silky. The use of turmeric and yellow chilli powder (famous from Lucknow) highlights the colour of the dish.

STAGE 1

3 tablespoons vegetable
or sunflower oil

2 red onions, sliced

8 green cardamom pods

2 mace threads

130 g (4½ oz/½ cup) plain thick
yoghurt, beaten

1½ tablespoons finely grated ginger

1 tablespoon crushed garlic

1½ teaspoons ground turmeric

1 teaspoon yellow chilli powder
(see glossary) or red chilli powder

4 lamb shanks, cut into 2 cm (¾ inch)
rounds (ask your butcher to do this)

2 small green chillies

STAGE 2

100 g (3½ oz) cashew nuts

3 tablespoons ghee (see glossary)

5 small green chillies, sliced

1 teaspoon Kashmiri chilli powder
(see glossary)

⅛ teaspoon ground cardamom

6 drops kewra water (pandanus water)
(see glossary)

5 saffron threads

3 tablespoons thin (pouring) cream

For stage 1, heat the oil in a heavy-based saucepan over medium heat, add the onion, cardamom and mace threads and cook for 6–8 minutes or until the onion is golden brown.

Reduce the heat to very low and while whisking, gradually add the yoghurt to prevent it from splitting (see tip).

Add the ginger and garlic and cook for 1 minute. Add the turmeric, chilli powder, lamb, green chillies and 2 litres (70 fl oz) of water and cook, covered, for 1 hour or until the lamb is tender.

Remove the lamb from the sauce, set aside and keep warm. Strain the sauce through a fine mesh sieve into a bowl, discarding the solids. Set aside and keep warm.

For stage 2, while the lamb is cooking, soak the cashew nuts in 500 ml (17 fl oz/2 cups) of hot water for 1 hour, then drain and rinse the nuts.

Put half into a spice grinder with 125 ml (4 fl oz/ ½ cup) of water and grind into a very smooth paste like smooth peanut butter. It's very important to the finished dish that this is very finely ground. Remove and set aside. Repeat with the remaining nuts and another 125 ml (4 fl oz/½ cup) of water. Set aside.

Heat the ghee in a clean heavy-based saucepan over low heat, add the cashew nut paste and cook for 3 minutes, stirring constantly as it tends to stick to the base of the pan. It's important to cook the paste over low heat so it gets cooked but doesn't burn.

Add the cooked lamb and strained sauce from stage 1 along with the green chilli, chilli powder, cardamom, kewra water, saffron and cream and stir to combine. Serve immediately.

Tip: When adding the yoghurt, the heat must not be high otherwise the yoghurt will split.

kola urundai kurma

lamb meatballs in coconut curry

65 g (2¼ oz/¾ cup) desiccated coconut

1 tablespoon poppy seeds

80 ml (2½ fl oz/⅓ cup) vegetable or sunflower oil

3 green cardamom pods

5 whole cloves

1 cinnamon stick

1 dried bay leaf

1 large onion, sliced

1 tablespoon finely grated ginger

1 tablespoon crushed garlic

1 teaspoon ground turmeric

2 teaspoons red chilli powder

1 tablespoon ground coriander

2 tomatoes, roughly chopped

95 g (3¼ oz/⅓ cup) plain thick yoghurt, beaten

coriander (cilantro) leaves, to garnish

fried onions, to garnish

MEATBALLS

800 g (1 lb 12 oz) lean minced (ground) lamb

3 small green chillies, chopped

½ bunch coriander (cilantro), leaves roughly chopped

½ bunch mint, leaves roughly chopped

2 tablespoons cashew nuts, roughly chopped

2 teaspoons finely grated ginger

½ teaspoon ground turmeric

30 ml (1 fl oz) lime juice

1 egg

Soak the coconut and poppy seeds in 250 ml
(9 fl oz/1 cup) of water for 20 minutes.

Meanwhile, to make the meatballs, combine
all of the ingredients in a bowl and roll into about
20 balls. Set aside.

Put the coconut mixture in a spice grinder with
the soaking water and grind together to form a
smooth paste — you may need to do this in several
batches (see tip). Set aside.

Heat the oil in a medium saucepan over medium
heat, add the cardamom, cloves, cinnamon stick,
bay leaf and onion and cook for 6–8 minutes or
until the onion is brown. Add the ginger and garlic
and cook for 2 minutes.

Combine the turmeric, chilli powder and ground
coriander with 3 tablespoons of water to make a
paste, then add to the pan, along with the tomato
and cook for 5 minutes.

Reduce the heat to low, stir in the beaten yoghurt,
coconut paste and 250 ml (9 fl oz/1 cup) of water
and cook for 5 minutes, being careful that the
yoghurt doesn't split (see tip). Season well with salt.

Add the meatballs, gradually stir in 250 ml
(9 fl oz/1 cup) of water and cook, covered, over
low heat, for 20–25 minutes or until the meatballs
are cooked. Ensure the sauce completely covers the
meatballs, adding more water if necessary. Serve
garnished with the coriander leaves and fried onions.

Tip: It is vital that the coconut is ground well
with the water as this acts as the binding agent in
the dish. If it isn't blended sufficiently, the dish will
separate and not thicken.

When adding the yoghurt, the heat must not
be high otherwise the yoghurt will split.

fried masala fish

1 x 500–600 g (1 lb 2 oz–1 lb 5 oz) whole snapper, cleaned, gutted and scaled (see tip)

juice of 2 limes

3 tablespoons fine rice flour

2 tablespoons vegetable oil

fried curry leaves, to garnish

black salt, to garnish (optional)

MASALA PASTE

2 tablespoons Kashmiri chilli powder (see glossary)

2 teaspoons sweet paprika

2 teaspoons ground cumin

1 teaspoon ground black pepper

½ teaspoon ground turmeric

1 tablespoon finely grated ginger

2 teaspoons crushed garlic

100 ml (3½ fl oz) gingili (unscented sesame oil) (see glossary)

SERVES 2 AS PART OF A SHARED MEAL

Preheat the oven to 170°C (325°F/Gas 3).

Wash the fish thoroughly in water to get rid of any excess scales. Score the fish diagonally on both sides to form a chequered pattern, so the masala can seep inside the fish. Pour the lime juice over the fish and set aside for 10 minutes.

Combine all of the masala paste ingredients in a bowl to form a smooth paste (do not add any water).

Coat the fish all over with the masala paste, then dust the fish in the rice flour.

Heat the oil in a heavy-based ovenproof frying pan over medium–low heat (see tip), add the fish and cook for 2 minutes each side to seal.

Transfer the pan to the oven and bake for 8 minutes or until the fish is just cooked through. Cut into large pieces to serve.

Serve garnished with the fried curry leaves and black salt.

Tip: Traditionally the fish used in this recipe is pomfret, which is occasionally available from select fishmongers. Whole silver dory or fillets of ocean perch or blue-eye trevalla are also good in this dish.

Cooking on high heat will burn the rice flour and the chilli powder.

kori gazi

mangalore chicken curry

Mrs Shetty of Mangalore, a family friend, visited us in Sydney and enjoyed my cooking. In return she shared her family secret to this dish. The effort of roasting spices individually for this dish makes all the difference. Many commercial versions of this dish are available, but this is her home-style treasure.

1½ tablespoons coriander seeds

½ teaspoon black peppercorns

¼ teaspoon fenugreek seeds

1 teaspoon cumin seeds

¼ teaspoon chilli flakes

100 g (3½ oz) desiccated coconut

¼ teaspoon ground turmeric

80 ml (2½ fl oz/⅓ cup) vegetable or sunflower oil

10 garlic cloves, sliced

3 onions, sliced

2 tablespoons tamarind pulp (see glossary)

80 ml (2½ fl oz/⅓ cup) coconut milk

1 kg (2 lb 4 oz) skinless, boneless chicken thigh fillets, diced

30 g (1 oz) ghee (see glossary)

10 curry leaves

SERVES 6–8 AS PART OF A SHARED MEAL

Heat a dry frying pan over medium heat, add the coriander seeds and cook, stirring regularly until lightly toasted and aromatic. Remove from the pan and set aside. Repeat separately with the black peppercorns, fenugreek seeds, cumin seeds and chilli flakes.

In the same pan, toast the coconut to a light golden colour. Transfer the coconut to a spice grinder with the toasted spices, turmeric and 125–250 ml (4–9 fl oz/½–1 cup) of water and grind to a fine paste — you will need to do this in several batches to ensure it is fine, which is important.

Heat the oil in a heavy-based saucepan over medium heat, add the garlic (reserving 1 teaspoon for finishing) and cook for 1 minute. Add the onion and cook for 10 minutes or until golden brown.

Stir in the coconut and spice paste, tamarind pulp and coconut milk. Add the chicken and cook, covered, over low heat for 20–25 minutes, stirring occasionally.

To finish, heat the ghee in a small frying pan over low heat, add the reserved garlic and the curry leaves and cook for 30 seconds, then pour the mixture over the chicken. Check the seasoning and serve immediately.

tabak maaz

crispy milk-poached lamb ribs

On one of my visits to Delhi, I got to taste this fabulous Kashmiri preparation at a place called Ahad Sons. It is a simple takeaway shop, which serves some of the most amazing Kashmiri food in Delhi. Kashmiri cuisine has been relatively unexplored in mainstream Indian cooking but it offers some very rich, flavoursome dishes involving some great cooking techniques and unusual ingredients. Tabak maaz is a speciality served at festive Wazwan banquets.

500 ml (17 fl oz/2 cups) milk

12 lamb ribs, cut into 3-rib pieces

1 teaspoon aniseed

2 teaspoons ground ginger

½ teaspoon ground turmeric

6 whole cloves

2 dried bay leaves

½ teaspoon black cumin seeds
(see glossary)

2 black cardamom pods

ghee (see glossary),
for shallow-frying

½ teaspoon amchur (dry mango
powder) (see glossary)

½ teaspoon Kashmiri chilli
powder (see glossary)

¼ teaspoon Kashmiri
garam masala (see glossary)

store-bought Indian pickled onions
and parathas (see glossary),
to serve

SERVES 4–6 AS A SNACK OR STARTER

Put the milk, lamb, aniseed, ginger, turmeric, cloves, bay leaves, cumin and cardamom in a heavy-based saucepan and bring to the boil, then reduce the heat to a simmer and cook, uncovered, for about 20 minutes or until the milk evaporates and the meat is tender, ensuring the base of the pan does not burn. Add 125 ml (4 fl oz/½ cup) of water during the cooking, if required.

Allow the lamb to cool to room temperature and scrape off any whole spices sticking to the meat.

Heat some ghee in a large deep-sided frying pan over medium heat, add the lamb and shallow-fry until crisp all over. The aim is to get a crisp exterior while the meat remains tender and juicy inside.

Combine the amchur, chilli powder and garam masala and sprinkle over the ribs. Serve hot with pickled onions and parathas.

arikadukka

steamed stuffed mussels

I ate these green lip mussels in Thalassery (Tellicherry), a coastal town in the north of Kerala. I was intrigued by this fascinating technique of first steaming and then frying the mussels.

180 g (6½ oz/¾ cup) grated coconut (see glossary)

¾ teaspoon cumin seeds

¾ teaspoon aniseed

2 green cardamom pods

360 g (12¾ oz/1½ cups) white iddiappam flour (see glossary)

vegetable or sunflower oil, for shallow-frying

9 French shallots (eschalots), chopped

25 green lip mussels

½ teaspoon garam masala

½ teaspoon red chilli powder

fried curry leaves, to garnish

SERVES 6 AS PART OF A SHARED MEAL

Put the coconut, cumin seeds, aniseed and cardamom in a spice grinder and grind to a fine paste.

Put 375 ml (13 fl oz/1½ cups) of water in a saucepan, bring to the boil, then add the iddiappam flour and stir until it is a thick dough. Add the coconut mixture and cook for 2 minutes. Remove from the heat and set aside to cool. This should feel like a soft gnocchi-like dough.

Heat 1 tablespoon of oil in a small frying pan over medium heat, add the shallot and cook until light brown. Drain on paper towel to remove any excess oil, then add to the dough. Set aside.

Scrub the mussels and pull out the hairy beards. Discard any that are broken. If there are any open ones, give them a tap on the bench and if they do not close, discard them. Lightly steam the mussels in a saucepan with about 5 cm (2 inches) of boiling water, until they just open. Drain and when cool enough to handle, carefully pry open the mussels, using the edge of a butter knife, making sure the two shells remain attached. Carefully remove the mussel meat, reserving the shells. Wrap each mussel with some of the dough, return to the shells and clean off any excess dough hanging outside the shells.

Line a metal or bamboo steamer basket with baking paper to prevent sticking. Put the mussels in a single layer in the basket, cover with a tight-fitting lid and steam over a saucepan or wok of simmering water for 20 minutes. Remove from the heat and allow to cool. Once the mussels cool down, the dough will have set over the mussel meat. Remove the dough-encased mussels from the shells.

Heat the oil in a deep-sided frying pan over medium–high heat, add the mussels and shallow-fry until golden brown all over. Remove from the pan, drain on paper towel and sprinkle over the garam masala and chilli powder, then garnish with curry leaves.

scampi ajadhina

pan-grilled scampi

8 scampi, unshelled

1 teaspoon ground turmeric

juice of 1 lime

3 tablespoons vegetable
or sunflower oil

a few drops of curry leaf–infused
oil (see page 188)

(see page 188)

SPICE POWDER

45 g (1½ oz/½ cup) desiccated
coconut

2 garlic cloves, roughly chopped

2 dried red chillies

2 teaspoons Kashmiri chilli powder
(see glossary)

2 teaspoons coriander seeds

½ teaspoon carom seeds (ajwain)
(see glossary)

¼ teaspoon cumin seeds

¼ teaspoon ground turmeric

2 teaspoons tamarind pulp
(see glossary)

SERVES 4 AS A STARTER

Preheat the oven to 180°C (350°F/Gas 4).

To make the spice powder, heat a dry frying pan over medium–high heat, add all of the ingredients, except the tamarind and lightly toast for about 1 minute, shaking the pan regularly. Transfer to a spice grinder with the tamarind pulp, season with salt and coarsely grind (see tip).

To prepare the scampi, snip off any very long legs using a sharp knife. Carefully butterfly each scampi slicing through the back shell and remove the intestinal vein. Rub the scampi with the turmeric and 2 teaspoons of the lime juice.

Heat 2 tablespoons of the vegetable oil in an ovenproof frying pan, add the scampi, flesh side down, and cook for 30 seconds to lightly sear.

Turn over the scampi, drizzle over the remaining oil, sprinkle with about half of the spice powder and immediately put the pan in the oven and roast for 5–7 minutes.

Drizzle with the curry leaf–infused oil and remaining lime juice and serve hot.

Tip: You can store the spice powder in an airtight jar in the fridge for up to 1 week. Use the remaining spice powder as a rub for fish.

tok jhol

sour fish curry

1 teaspoon ground turmeric

1 tablespoon vegetable or sunflower oil

400 g (14 oz) garfish, bone from head removed (ask your fishmonger to do this), cut into bite-sized pieces

4 small green chillies, roughly chopped

3 tablespoons tamarind pulp (see glossary)

½ teaspoon grated palm sugar (jaggery) or soft brown sugar

TEMPERING

2 teaspoons mustard oil (see glossary)

2 teaspoons panch phoran masala (see glossary)

1½ tablespoons chickpea flour (besan)

Combine ½ teaspoon of salt with ½ teaspoon of the turmeric and 1 teaspoon of the oil. Rub all over the fish and set aside for 30 minutes.

Put the chilli in a small blender or spice grinder and grind to a coarse paste.

To make the tempering, heat the mustard oil in a small frying pan over high heat until just smoking, add the panch phoran masala and allow it to crackle. Add the chickpea flour and cook for 10 seconds. Remove from the heat and set aside.

Combine 1 teaspoon of the oil, the remaining turmeric, the tamarind pulp, palm sugar, the green chilli paste and a pinch of salt in a large bowl. Add the fish and the tempering and mix well.

Heat the remaining oil in a frying pan over medium heat. Add the fish mixture and 125 ml (4 fl oz/½ cup) of water and cook, covered, for about 5 minutes or until the fish is cooked, adding a little extra water if necessary. The sauce should be like a thick gravy. If it is a little thin, remove the fish from the pan, then cook the sauce, uncovered, for 1–2 minutes to thicken. Check the seasoning and serve.

nalli gosht patiala

lamb shanks patiala

90 ml (3 fl oz) vegetable
or sunflower oil

3 black cardamom pods

6 green cardamom pods

2.5 cm (1 inch) piece of
cinnamon stick

1 teaspoon black cumin seeds

8 whole cloves

2 onions, sliced

1 tablespoon finely grated ginger

1 tablespoon crushed garlic

½ teaspoon ground turmeric

2 teaspoons red chilli powder

1½ tablespoons ground coriander

4–6 lamb shanks, cut into 2 cm
(¾ inch) rounds (ask your butcher
to do this)

125 g (4½ oz/½ cup) tomato
paste (concentrated purée)

¼ teaspoon ground mace

¼ teaspoon grated nutmeg

2 tablespoons roughly chopped
coriander (cilantro)

parathas or rotis (see glossary),
to serve

SERVES 6 AS PART OF A SHARED MEAL

Heat the oil in a large heavy-based casserole dish over medium–high heat, add the cardamom, cinnamon stick, cumin and cloves and cook for 1–2 minutes or until fragrant. Add the onion and cook for 5 minutes or until golden. Stir in the ginger and garlic and cook for 2 minutes, sprinkling with 1 tablespoon of water, if necessary, to prevent it burning. Add the turmeric, chilli powder and ground coriander and cook for 2 minutes.

Add the lamb, stir to coat in the spices and cook for 2 minutes or until sealed on all sides.

Add the tomato paste and 1 litre (35 fl oz/4 cups) of water and cook, covered, over low heat for 1–1½ hours, adding extra water if the sauce evaporates too quickly. The meat should be almost falling off the bone. Stir in the mace and nutmeg, season with salt and remove from the heat. Garnish with the chopped coriander and serve with hot parathas or rotis.

nandu milagu masala

coconut chilli crab

1 x 1 kg (2 lb 4 oz) live mud crab

2 tablespoons vegetable or
sunflower oil

1 large onion, sliced

2 dried Kashmiri chillies
(see glossary)

2 teaspoons finely grated ginger

2 teaspoons crushed garlic

1 tomato, chopped

3 tablespoons coconut cream

curry leaves, to garnish (optional)

MASALA PASTE

150 g (5½ oz) grated coconut
(see glossary) or desiccated
coconut

6 dried Kashmiri chillies
(see glossary) or 1½ tablespoons
hot paprika

1 teaspoon black peppercorns

1 tablespoon coriander seeds

2 teaspoons cumin seeds

1 teaspoon ground turmeric

SERVES 4 AS PART OF A SHARED MEAL

Carefully place the crab in the freezer for 1 hour to put it to sleep. To prepare the crab, pull off the top shell and set aside. Remove and discard the feathery gills on either side. Using a meat cleaver or large knife, cut the crab into quarters with legs attached. Cut off each claw. Lightly crush the shell of the claws and legs with the back of the knife.

To make the masala paste, put all of the ingredients in a spice grinder and process until fine. Remove half from the grinder and set aside. Add 3 tablespoons of water to the grinder and blend to form a very smooth, fine paste. Remove from the grinder and set aside. Repeat with the remaining ground spices.

Heat the oil in a large heavy-based saucepan over medium heat, add the onion and chillies and cook for about 5 minutes. Add the ginger and garlic and cook for 2 minutes. Add the masala paste and cook for 2 minutes.

Add 500 ml (17 fl oz/2 cups) of water and the tomato and simmer over low heat for 15 minutes, adding the coconut cream towards the end of the cooking time.

Add the crab claws and cook for 5 minutes, then add the remaining crab pieces, adding a little more water, if necessary. Cook, covered, for about 3 minutes or until the crab is cooked through. Scatter over the curry leaves to garnish.

kakori kebabs

minced lamb kebabs

The opulence of the royals' day starts with rich kebabs. They are meant to give them energy for the day. The meat is passed through a meat mincer a couple of times to make a fine paste, so the texture of the cooked kebab is almost like pâté. Due to the high fat content of the ground meat, it needs to set and chill in the fridge before you can mould it onto the skewers and cook it.

3 tablespoons chickpea
flour (besan)

1 teaspoon yellow chilli powder
(see glossary)

½ teaspoon ground mace

1 teaspoon ground cardamom

½ teaspoon ground white pepper

1 kg (2 lb 4 oz) finely minced
(ground) lamb (passed through
a meat mincer twice)

270 g (9½ oz) ghee (see glossary)

1½ tablespoons finely
grated ginger

1 tablespoon crushed garlic

1 teaspoon garam masala

green chutney (see page 210),
to serve

MAKES 10–12 / SERVES 5–6 AS PART OF A SHARED MEAL

Heat a small dry frying pan over medium–high heat, add the chickpea flour and lightly toast, shaking the pan regularly. Combine with the chilli powder, mace, cardamom and pepper and set aside.

Combine the lamb with the ghee, ginger, garlic and garam masala in a large bowl and knead to a doughy consistency. As you knead, the colour of the meat will become paler and lighter. Add the chickpea flour mixture and knead to combine well. Put in the fridge for 1 hour to firm up.

Divide the mixture into 10–12 portions and, with slightly wet hands, mould the mixture onto metal skewers.

Preheat a charcoal barbecue or regular barbecue grill plate to medium heat. Cook the skewers for 8–10 minutes or until browned and cooked through — the cooking time will depend on how close the kebabs are to the heat. Serve with the chutney.

seafood panch phoran

five-spice seafood curry

1 kg (2 lb 4 oz) ripe roma
(plum) tomatoes

2 tablespoons sunflower oil

6 dried red chillies

1 teaspoon panch phoran masala
(see glossary)

1 red onion, diced

½ teaspoon red chilli powder

1 tablespoon finely grated ginger

1 kg (2 lb 4 oz) mixed seafood,
such as scallops, prawns (shrimp),
white fish pieces and calamari

6 coriander (cilantro) sprigs, leaves
roughly chopped

1 tablespoon finely shredded
ginger

SERVES 6–8 AS PART OF A SHARED MEAL

Score a shallow cross in the base of the tomatoes. Put in a heatproof bowl and cover with boiling water. Leave for 30 seconds, then transfer to cold water and peel the skin away from the cross. Cut the tomatoes in half, scoop out the seeds with a teaspoon and discard. Roughly chop the flesh and set aside.

Heat the oil in a frying pan over medium–high heat, add the dried chillies and cook until the tips of the chillies turn black. Add the panch phoran masala and cook for 1–2 minutes.

Add the onion and cook over medium–low heat for 5 minutes or until soft and translucent but without browning. Add the chilli powder, ginger and tomato and cook for 15 minutes.

Add the seafood, increase the heat to medium and cook for 3 minutes or until the seafood is cooked. Serve garnished with the coriander and ginger.

Tip: The sweetness of the seafood is enhanced with the sweetness of the tomato while the panch phoran masala gives the dish its balance.

whole snapper recheado

spice-crusted whole snapper

2 small snapper, cleaned, gutted and scaled

3 tablespoons vegetable or sunflower oil

thinly sliced red onion, to garnish

fried onions, to garnish

MASALA PASTE

6 dried Kashmiri chillies (see glossary)

1 onion, roughly chopped

6 garlic cloves, roughly chopped

5 cm (2 inch) piece of ginger, roughly chopped

10 black peppercorns

4 whole cloves

2.5 cm (1 inch) piece of cassia bark (see glossary)

½ teaspoon cumin seeds

¼ teaspoon ground turmeric

80 ml (2½ fl oz/⅓ cup) toddy vinegar (see glossary), malt vinegar or palm vinegar (see glossary)

SERVES 4–6 AS PART OF A SHARED MEAL

Preheat the oven to 180°C (350°F/Gas 4).

To make the masala paste, put all of the ingredients in a blender, season with salt and blend to a smooth paste.

Wash the fish thoroughly in water to get rid of any excess scales. Score the fish with three diagonal cuts on both sides, so the masala can seep inside the fish. Rub the masala paste all over the fish.

Heat the oil in a large ovenproof frying pan over medium–high heat, add the fish and cook briefly on both sides to seal. Cover with foil (to prevent the masala crust burning), put the pan in the oven and roast for 5 minutes, then remove the foil and roast for a further 5–10 minutes or until the fish is just cooked.

Garnish with the sliced red and fried onion and drizzle over some of the pan juices to serve.

jhinge aloo posto

ridge gourd & potato

*My head chef at Abhi's, Ranjan Choudhury, served us this beautiful dish for a lunch at his house.
Even though it was specially prepared for Suba, being a vegetarian, I, the carnivore, couldn't
keep my hands off it and Suba's plate too! Posto refers to white poppy seeds, which is a
prominent ingredient in Bengali cooking.*

**100 g (3½ oz) white poppy seeds
(see glossary)**

3–4 small green chillies, chopped

**500 g (1 lb 2 oz) ridge gourd
(loofah)**

**80 ml (2½ fl oz/⅓ cup) vegetable
or sunflower oil**

**½ teaspoon nigella seeds (onion
seeds/kalonji) (see glossary)**

1 onion, sliced

**2 waxy potatoes, cut into 3 cm
(1¼ inch) cubes**

¼ teaspoon ground turmeric

Soak the poppy seeds in 3 tablespoons of water for 20 minutes.
Put the seeds and soaking water in a small blender with two-thirds
of the chilli and process to a fine paste.

Peel the ridges off the ridge gourd, removing the tough green
outer layer to get a smooth surface. Halve the gourd lengthways,
then slice fairly thickly into half moons. Set aside.

Heat the oil in a medium saucepan over medium heat, add the
nigella seeds and cook for 30 seconds, then add the onion and
cook for 3 minutes.

Add the potato, turmeric, remaining green chilli and the poppy
seed paste, sprinkle with 1 tablespoon of water and cook until
the potato is well coated with the poppy seed paste. Stir in 80 ml
(2½ fl oz/⅓ cup) of water and cook, covered, for 8 minutes,
stirring regularly or until the potato is half cooked.

Add the ridge gourd and cook for 5–7 minutes, stirring
regularly. Season with salt and serve hot.

chicken chettiyar milagu

tomato & pepper chicken curry

A delicious Chettinad dish, where the use of tomatoes and pepper play dominant roles, without the use of coconut. This dish is cooked best by my youngest chef, Vikram Arumugam, who is a Chettiyar boy, and has been an integral part of Aki's since we opened.

3 tablespoons vegetable
or sunflower oil

1 teaspoon black mustard seeds

2 dried red chillies

¼ teaspoon fenugreek seeds

½ teaspoon cumin seeds

1 cinnamon stick

2 green cardamom pods

4 whole cloves

¼ teaspoon fennel seeds

1 onion, thinly sliced

1½ tablespoons finely grated
ginger

1½ tablespoons crushed garlic

1½ teaspoons ground turmeric

1 tablespoon red chilli powder

2½ tablespoons ground coriander

200 g (7 oz) tomatoes, diced

4 small green chillies, halved
lengthways

1 kg (2 lb 4 oz) chicken thigh fillets,
each cut into 3

2 teaspoons cracked
black pepper

10 curry leaves

SERVES 6 AS PART OF A SHARED MEAL

Heat the oil in a large heavy-based saucepan over medium heat, add the mustard seeds and let them crackle for about 20 seconds. Add the red chillies, fenugreek and cumin and cook for 1 minute. Add the cinnamon, cardamom, cloves and fennel and cook for 1 minute.

Add the onion and cook for 6–8 minutes, stirring occasionally until almost golden brown. Add the ginger, garlic and 1 teaspoon of water and cook for 1 minute.

Add the turmeric, chilli powder and coriander and cook for 2 minutes, sprinkling with 1–2 tablespoons of water to prevent the mixture burning.

Add the tomato, green chilli and chicken and cook for 5 minutes or until the juices start to release from the chicken.

Add 375 ml (13 fl oz/1½ cups) of water and cook, covered, over low heat, for about 20 minutes or until the chicken is cooked through. Season with salt if necessary, then finish with the pepper and curry leaves.

Tip: Coriander (cilantro) leaves aren't normally added to this dish as they are too strong.

fish tikka

grilled swordfish

2 teaspoons finely grated ginger

2 teaspoons crushed garlic

¼ teaspoon ground turmeric

½ teaspoon red chilli powder

2 tablespoons malt vinegar

¼ teaspoon garam masala

2 tablespoons chana dal (see glossary), toasted and finely ground, or toasted chickpea flour (besan)

⅛ teaspoon carom seeds (ajwain) (see glossary)

2 tablespoons mustard oil (see glossary)

600 g (1 lb 5 oz) swordfish steaks, cut into 6 portions

vegetable or sunflower oil, for brushing

green chutney (see page 210), to serve

SERVES 6 AS PART OF A SHARED MEAL

Combine all of the ingredients, except the fish, oil and chutney. Rub all over the fish and set aside to marinate for 30 minutes.

Preheat a barbecue grill plate or hotplate. Lightly brush with oil and grill the fish for 2 minutes on one side, then turn over and cook the other side for 2 minutes or until just cooked through. Serve with the green chutney.

sweet

A HAPPY FAMILY IS A SWEET BALANCE. Our boys, Abhi and Aki, who our restaurants are named after, are the ultimate 'sweet' for us. Our desire for the restaurants to be successful has meant that our family spend a lot of time there. If you ask either Abhi or Aki, 'What is family time?', I am sure they will answer, 'The restaurant Abhi's.' For all the missed homework, soccer goals and dinner-time conversations, rather than resent the hours that the business took away from family time, Abhi and Aki have come to love the restaurants and are involved in day-to-day operations. We could not have asked for a sweeter ending.

In India, every happy moment is celebrated by sharing sweets. At festive occasions, weddings and religious ceremonies, sweets are often served before any other foods. Indians believe, poetically, that by starting a meal sweetly life will also continue that way. In a Southern Indian wedding, for example, food is served on banana leaves and strict rules govern where food is put. Sweet things are always on the right-hand side, roughly at the four o'clock, which is where you start eating the meal in an anti-clockwise direction. It's the same for thali plates across India — you always eat the sweet first.

When I met my wife, Suba, for the first time, it was over sweets. It's traditional for the bride's family to serve kesari (semolina cake), and Suba's mother made pineapple kesari (see page 205 for a recipe), that I loved so much I asked for seconds.

India even has its own version of Mr Whippy to excite children, the kulfiwalla, who pushes his cart filled with kulfis, which come in a long conical shape with a paddle-pop stick.

Others sweets, such as halwa, are ubiquitous, yet differ between regions. In Mumbai (Bombay), the halwa is hard and caramelly and cut into cubes, while in the south it's softer and needs to be scooped. I'm proud to say my home of Tirunelveli in Tamil Nadu, makes the most popular halwa in India. It has the consistency of Turkish delight and people come from all over to buy it from confectioner Iruttu Kadai Halwa. Making it is so laborious that my mother didn't believe it was worthwhile teaching Suba how to do it. Thankfully, my mum still makes it for me when I go to visit the family.

Of course, as much as we love them, sweets should be eaten in moderation — an excess causes discontent and yearning, while just the right amount promises satisfaction and longevity.

pistachio kulfi

pistachio ice cream

Kulfi is a very popular North Indian ice cream consumed by all. Traditionally it is served on wooden sticks by street hawkers. Eating kulfi takes Suba back to her childhood days. Back in the 1970s in India, she did not have the luxury of owning a fridge, so her after-school treat on hot days would be kulfi. When she heard the kulfiwalla's bell in the street, she knew 'heaven on a stick' was just outside.

The secret of a good kulfi is in the slow freezing — it should not have crystallised icicles. This is achieved by reducing the milk to a nice thick consistency thereby removing the water from the milk. Today, we have evaporated milk, which is the closest to reduced milk. This recipe uses evaporated milk but if you feel adventurous, you can use full-cream milk and slowly reduce it to a third. The kulfi survives well in the freezer and can be prepared in bulk and kept for a long time.

750 ml (26 fl oz/3 cups) evaporated milk

120 ml (4 fl oz) thickened (whipping) cream

120 g (4¼ oz) white sugar

5 tablespoons pistachio kernels, coarsely crushed, plus extra to garnish

½ teaspoon ground cardamom

STRAWBERRY COULIS

100 g (3½ oz) strawberries, diced

30 g (1 oz) caster (superfine) sugar

1 star anise

½ cinnamon stick

SERVES 6 AS A DESSERT

Put the milk, cream and sugar in a heavy-based saucepan over low heat and cook for 20 minutes, scraping down the sides of the pan regularly.

Add 3 tablespoons of the crushed pistachios and the ground cardamom, then remove from the heat. Press a piece of plastic wrap onto the surface of the milk mixture and set aside to cool.

Pour into takeaway containers (either three larger ones or six smaller ones) or six 125 ml (4 fl oz/½ cup) capacity dariole moulds. Cover with the lids or tightly with plastic wrap to prevent crystallisation. Put in the freezer until frozen.

To make the strawberry coulis, put all of the ingredients in a saucepan with 125 ml (4 fl oz/½ cup) of water and cook over low heat for about 5 minutes. Once the strawberries are soft, discard the star anise and cinnamon stick and strain the mixture through a fine mesh sieve placed over a bowl. Using the back of a spoon, push the solids through to form a smooth coulis.

Remove the kulfi from the freezer about 10 minutes before serving, then turn out onto individual serving plates, serve with the strawberry coulis and garnish with the extra crushed pistachios.

Tip: Feel free to experiment with flavours. Some popular ones are rose, saffron, fig and walnut.

kadai mangai curry

quail with mango curry

4 butterflied quails

1 teaspoon ground turmeric

2 teaspoons finely grated ginger

1 tablespoon ghee (see glossary)

1 teaspoon cumin seeds

½ teaspoon red chilli powder

2 dried red chillies

**2 teaspoons tamarind pulp
(see glossary)**

**1 teaspoon coriander seeds,
crushed**

**1 tablespoon grated palm sugar
(jaggery) or soft brown sugar**

**1½ tablespoons store-bought sweet
mango chutney**

**2 tablespoons vegetable or
sunflower oil**

**3–4 fresh green mango slices
(optional)**

SERVES 4

Preheat the oven to 180°C (350°F/Gas 4) and put a baking tray in to heat up.

Rub the quail with a little salt and half of the turmeric and ginger. Set aside to rest for 20 minutes.

Heat the ghee in a frying pan over medium heat. Add the cumin seeds and gently cook for 1 minute. Add the chilli powder, dried chillies, tamarind pulp, coriander seeds and remaining turmeric and ginger and cook for 4 minutes. Season with salt and add the palm sugar and mango chutney and cook for 5–7 minutes, gradually adding about 185 ml (6 fl oz/¾ cup) of water until the sauce is thick enough to coat the quail. Keep warm and set aside.

Heat the oil in a large ovenproof frying pan over high heat, add the quails, skin side down, and sear for 2 minutes, then turn over and cook for a further 1 minute. Put the pan in the oven and roast for 4–6 minutes or until the quail is cooked but still moist inside — do not overcook.

Gently reheat the sauce if necessary. Cut each quail in half or quarters and drizzle the sauce over. Serve garnished with the mango.

Tip: If you don't have an ovenproof frying pan to cook the quail in, simply preheat a baking dish or baking tray in the oven and transfer the quail from the pan to the dish or tray to roast.

veal paṣanda

rolled veal in almond & saffron sauce

This dish was instrumental in Abhi's getting the recognition from the most important food critic of Sydney in 1994. It is tender veal slices, rolled with sultanas, cashews and pistachios then simmered in a rich saffron and almond sauce.

6 veal slices (scalloppini)

3 tablespoons slivered almonds

2 tablespoons cashew nuts

1 tablespoon finely grated ginger

1 tablespoon crushed garlic

2 tablespoons ghee (see glossary)

3 tablespoons vegetable
or sunflower oil

3–4 green cardamom pods

1 teaspoon red chilli powder

2 teaspoons ground coriander

10 saffron threads

2 red onions, sliced

150 g (5½ oz) plain thick
yoghurt, beaten

100 ml (3½ fl oz) thin
(pouring) cream

2 teaspoons roughly chopped
coriander (cilantro)

FILLING

1½ tablespoons milk powder

1 tablespoon coriander (cilantro)
leaves, chopped

1 tablespoon crushed cashew nuts

2 teaspoons pistachio nuts, halved,
plus extra, crushed, to garnish

2 teaspoons sultanas (golden raisins),
roughly chopped

¼ teaspoon ground cardamom

Combine all of the filling ingredients in a bowl, then divide into six portions.

Lay the veal slices on a work surface. Place a portion of filling in the centre of each, leaving the edges clear. Fold in two opposite sides over the filling, then begin rolling from an open side and roll up the veal tightly like a spring roll, making sure all sides are sealed. Refrigerate for 4 hours.

Meanwhile, soak the almonds and cashew nuts in a bowl of hot water for 1 hour. Drain, then put in a spice grinder and grind into a smooth paste. Set aside.

Combine the ginger and garlic.

Heat the ghee and 1 tablespoon of the oil together in a saucepan over medium heat, add the cardamom, chilli powder, ground coriander and saffron, and when fragrant, add the onion and cook until golden brown. Add the ginger–garlic paste and fry for 2 minutes.

Mix the beaten yoghurt with the cashew and almond paste, add to the pan and cook over low heat for 20 minutes, adding 80–250 ml (2½–9 fl oz/ ⅓–1 cup) of water sparingly in stages. Once the oil starts to separate, remove the pan from the heat.

Heat the remaining oil in a large frying pan over medium–high heat, add the veal rolls and cook briefly on all sides, adding a little salt to taste (see tip).

Pour the sauce over the veal and cook for 2 minutes. Stir in the cream and serve garnished with the chopped coriander.

Tip: As veal is a prime cut of meat with little fat, it cooks quickly, so be careful not to overcook it and keep in mind that it will cook further in the sauce.

wagyu beef ullathu

keralan beef fry

This is a modern take on the traditional Keralan beef ullathu, using the great wagyu reared in Australia. There are a few steps in this recipe but it isn't laborious and the results are remarkable. Once the chickpeas are cooked, it is a quick and simple dish to make. The beef needs to be cooked just before serving and the dish finished at the last minute, so make sure you have everything ready.

95 g (3¼ oz/½ cup) black chickpeas (kala chana) (see glossary), soaked overnight and drained (or 220 g/7¾ oz tinned chickpeas, rinsed and drained)

1 teaspoon ground fennel

2 teaspoons ground black pepper

1 teaspoon ground turmeric

2 teaspoons red chilli powder

1 tablespoon ground coriander

80 ml (2½ fl oz/⅓ cup) vegetable or sunflower oil

juice of 1 lime

1 kg (2 lb 4 oz) wagyu beef, cut into 125 g (4½ oz) medallions

1 teaspoon black mustard seeds

1 teaspoon fennel seeds

2 teaspoons coriander seeds, coarsely crushed

6 dried red chillies

1 teaspoon black peppercorns, coarsely crushed

2 red onions, chopped

1 tablespoon finely grated ginger

1 tablespoon sliced garlic

3 tablespoons fresh coconut strips or dried coconut flakes

10 curry leaves

5 cm (2 inch) piece of ginger, finely shredded

You will need to begin this recipe 1 day ahead.

If using black chickpeas, cook in salted water over medium heat for about 2 hours or until tender. Drain and set aside. This can be done the day before and the chickpeas kept in the fridge. If using tinned chickpeas, do not cook.

Meanwhile, combine the ground fennel, ground pepper, turmeric, chilli powder, ground coriander, 1½ tablespoons of the oil and three-quarters of the lime juice in a small non-metallic bowl, rub the mixture all over the beef and leave to marinate in the fridge for 1 hour (see tip).

Heat the remaining oil in a frying pan over medium heat, add the mustard and fennel seeds and let them crackle for about 20 seconds. Add the coriander seeds, dried chillies and peppercorns and cook for 1 minute. Add the onion and cook for 6–8 minutes or until golden brown. Add the ginger and garlic and cook for 3 minutes.

Chargrill the beef as desired (preferably medium–rare to medium). Remove from the heat and set aside to rest.

Add the chickpeas and coconut strips to the onion mixture, increase the heat to high, add the beef, tossing to coat with the onion mixture, chickpeas and coconut strips. Toss until everything is combined and heated through, then remove from the heat and add the remaining lime juice and the curry leaves and ginger. Serve immediately.

Tip: Do not add salt to the marinade at this stage as it will dehydrate the meat.

wattalappam

jaggery baked custard

This dessert originates from the Keralite Muslim populace. It is now a popular Sri Lankan dessert. It is made with kithul jaggery, which is a dark brown and slightly bitter in taste, but when paired with the sweetness of the coconut milk, it provides a great balance of taste and colour.

110 g (3¾ oz/½ cup) white sugar

1 tablespoon cashew nuts, roughly chopped

500 ml (17 fl oz/2 cups) coconut milk

175 g (6 oz/1½ cups) grated kithul jaggery (see glossary)

½ teaspoon ground cardamom

¼ teaspoon ground mace

5 eggs, lightly beaten (see tip)

SERVES 8 AS A DESSERT

Preheat the oven to 160°C (315°F/Gas 2–3).

Put the sugar in a frying pan over medium–high heat and allow to melt, swirling the pan occasionally but do not stir. Cook until it is a light golden caramel, then quickly but carefully pour the caramel into eight 125 ml (4 fl oz/½ cup) capacity ramekins and swirl around to coat the base of the ramekins. Sprinkle the cashew nuts over the caramel. Set aside.

Put the coconut milk, jaggery, cardamom and mace in a large mixing bowl and beat well for 4–5 minutes or until the jaggery has dissolved. Stir in the eggs, then strain the mixture through a fine mesh sieve into a jug. Pour the liquid into the prepared ramekins and put in a roasting tray. Pour hot water into the tray to come about halfway up the sides of the ramekins.

Bake for 20 minutes, then reduce the oven temperature to 140°C (275°F/Gas 1) and bake for a further 15–20 minutes or until the wattalappam are set.

Remove from the oven and the water bath and cool, then refrigerate.

Bring to room temperature before serving. To remove the wattalappam, gently push down the sides of the custard to release it from the ramekin, then dip the ramekins in hot water and invert onto individual serving plates.

Tip: Do not aerate the eggs by beating them too much as a good wattalappam should have no air bubbles. It should resemble the texture of a crème caramel.

kanavai nerachathu

stuffed squid with spiced tomato coulis

12 baby squid

2 tablespoons vegetable oil

**baby coriander (cilantro) leaves,
to garnish**

1 tablespoon sunflower oil

½ teaspoon fennel seeds

3 dried red chillies

**90 g (3¼ oz/⅓ cup) tomato paste
(concentrated purée)**

**½ bunch coriander (cilantro),
leaves roughly chopped**

juice of 1 lime

STUFFING

1 tablespoon vegetable oil

**6 French shallots (eschalots),
finely chopped**

1 teaspoon chopped ginger

4 garlic cloves, crushed

**100 g (3½ oz) raw prawn (shrimp)
meat, chopped**

1 tomato, finely chopped

2 small green chillies, chopped

**½ bunch coriander (cilantro),
leaves roughly chopped**

**2 tablespoons chickpea flour
(besan)**

1 tablespoon tamarind pulp

½ teaspoon ground turmeric

SERVES 6 AS PART OF A SHARED MEAL

First clean the squid. Gently pull the tentacles away from the tube (the intestines should come away at the same time) and set aside. Remove the intestines from the tentacles by cutting under the eyes, then remove the beak, using your fingers to push up the centre. Reserve the tentacles. Pull away the quill (the transparent cartilage) from inside the body and remove. Remove and discard the white membrane from the body. Slice off the wings and reserve.

To make the stuffing, heat the oil in a frying pan over medium heat, add the shallot and cook, without browning, for 3 minutes. Add the ginger and garlic and cook for less than a minute. Add the remaining stuffing ingredients, including the squid wings, and cook over medium–high heat for 2 minutes or until you have a dry-ish mixture. Remove from the heat, season with salt and set aside to cool.

Stuff the squid tubes with the stuffing and skewer the openings with toothpicks to secure. Set aside.

To make the spiced tomato coulis, heat the oil in a small saucepan over medium heat, add the fennel and dried chillies and cook for 1 minute or until fragrant and the tips of the chillies blacken. Add the tomato paste and 250 ml (9 fl oz/1 cup) of water and cook over medium heat for 5–7 minutes. Stir in the coriander and lime juice and remove from the heat.

Meanwhile, heat the oil in a frying pan over high heat. Add the stuffed squid and tentacles and sear each side. This will only take a couple of minutes as the filling is already cooked and you only need to cook the outside — do not overcook the squid or they will become rubbery. Serve the squid immediately with a little of the coulis drizzled over the plate and garnished with the coriander leaves.

sand whiting caldin

goan fish curry

I ate this dish in a little shack in Goa called Filsumai. The Goan duo, Johnny Gonzalves and Aunty Lourds, run this little joint showcasing their great passion for Goan cuisine. This is my take on the fish caldin I had there.

4 whole sand whiting, cleaned, gutted and scaled

1½ teaspoons ground turmeric

3 tablespoons vegetable or sunflower oil

2 onions, chopped

2 small green chillies, halved lengthways

1 tomato, chopped

1 tablespoon tamarind pulp (see glossary)

80 ml (2½ fl oz/⅓ cup) coconut milk

PASTE

45 g (1½ oz/½ cup) desiccated coconut

4 garlic cloves, crushed

2 tablespoons coriander seeds

1 tablespoon finely grated ginger

1 tablespoon cumin seeds

1 tablespoon black peppercorns

3 dried red chillies

1 tablespoon white poppy seeds (see glossary)

SERVES 4 AS PART OF A SHARED MEAL

Cut each fish into three pieces. Rub with a little of the ground turmeric and set aside for 20 minutes.

To make the paste, place all of the ingredients in a small blender and process until finely ground. Add 125 ml (4 fl oz/ ½ cup) of water and blend to a smooth paste. Set aside.

Heat the oil in a heavy-based saucepan over medium heat, add the onion and cook for 6–8 minutes or until light brown. Add the chillies, tomato and prepared paste, stir and cook for 15 minutes or until the raw coconut smell is gone.

Add the fish, tamarind pulp and sufficient water to only just cover the fish, season with salt and cook for 5–7 minutes.

Add the coconut milk and cook for 5 minutes. Serve immediately.

Tip: The coconut milk is added towards the end so it retains its sweetness.

quail porichadu

pan-seared quail

1 tablespoon ground coriander

1 teaspoon ground cumin

½ teaspoon ground turmeric

1 teaspoon red chilli powder

1 teaspoon garam masala

juice of 1 lemon

1 tablespoon finely grated ginger

1 teaspoon crushed garlic

4 butterflied quails

3 tablespoons vegetable oil

1 teaspoon fennel seeds

2 dried red chillies

1 red onion, sliced

1 potato, thinly sliced

20 curry leaves

finely shredded ginger, to serve

SERVES 4 AS PART OF A SHARED MEAL

Preheat the oven to 180°C (350°F/Gas 4).

Combine the coriander, cumin, turmeric, chilli powder, garam masala, lemon juice, ginger and garlic and rub all over the quails. Set aside to marinate for 20 minutes.

Heat 1 tablespoon of the oil in a large ovenproof frying pan (see tip) over medium heat, add the fennel and chillies and cook until the tips of the chillies blacken. Add the onion and cook for 6–8 minutes or until golden brown.

While the onion is being cooked, heat 1 tablespoon of oil in a frying pan over medium–high heat and quickly fry the sliced potato. Set aside.

Add the quails, skin side down, to the pan with the onion and sear for 2 minutes, then turn over and sear for 1 minute. Towards the end, add half of the curry leaves and the fried potato and toss to combine.

Put the pan in the oven and roast 4–6 minutes or until the quail is cooked but still moist inside — do not overcook.

Meanwhile, heat the remaining oil in a frying pan over low heat, add the curry leaves and cook until just crisp. Drain on paper towel and set aside.

Serve the quail garnished with the fried curry leaves and ginger.

Tip: If you don't have an ovenproof frying pan to cook the quail in, simply preheat a baking dish or baking tray in the oven and transfer the quail mixture from the pan to the dish to roast.

lau chingri

school prawns with winter melon

I came across this dish through the Indian Consul General, Amit Dasgupta, a frequent diner at Aki's and a passionate food enthusiast. He enjoys sharing his culinary knowledge and has been kind enough to pass on his mother's recipe. I find this dish to have a lot of clean and simple flavours where the ingredients speak for themselves. It is a quick and easy dish to prepare and is one of my favourites. It's best cooked with small prawns. The traditional recipe asks for the prawns to be cooked whole because of the size. They are cooked to a crunchy texture and provide an excellent counterpoint to the melon.

100 ml (3½ fl oz) vegetable or sunflower oil, for shallow-frying

600 g (1 lb 5 oz) school prawns (shrimp), heads removed and legs trimmed

1 dried bay leaf

3 dried red chillies

½ teaspoon white sugar

1½ teaspoons panch phoran masala (see glossary)

1 tablespoon finely grated ginger

200 g (7 oz) winter melon, peeled, halved lengthways, seeds removed and sliced

2 teaspoons ground cumin

juice of 1 lime

SERVES 4–6 AS PART OF A SHARED MEAL

Heat the oil in a large deep-sided frying pan over high heat, add the prawns, in small batches, and shallow-fry until crisp. Remove with a slotted spoon and drain on paper towel. Set aside.

Discard all but 3 tablespoons of the oil in the pan and heat over medium heat. Add the bay leaf, dried chillies, sugar and panch phoran masala and cook for 1 minute. Stir in the ginger, add the winter melon and cook, covered, for about 10 minutes or until the winter melon is tender. Stir in the cumin.

Toss in the prawns, season with salt and increase the heat to evaporate any excess liquid. Add lime juice to taste and serve.

craб iддiappam

coconut crab with steamed rice noodle cakes

Iddiappam are also known as string hoppers in Sri Lankan cooking. You will need speciality iddiappam flour and an iddiappam mould (or a pasta machine). These are both available from Indian and Sri Lankan grocery stores.

COCONUT BROTH

1 tomato

1 tablespoon vegetable
or sunflower oil

½ teaspoon black mustard seeds

½ teaspoon fennel seeds

½ teaspoon fenugreek seeds

1 red onion, thinly sliced

2 small green chillies,
halved lengthways

½ teaspoon ground turmeric

6 curry leaves

1 teaspoon finely grated ginger

330 ml (11¼ fl oz/1⅓ cups)
coconut milk

CRAB TOPPING

2 teaspoons vegetable
or sunflower oil

1 teaspoon black
mustard seeds

1 teaspoon finely grated ginger

½ teaspoon fennel seeds

2 red onions, finely chopped

1 small green chilli, chopped

½ teaspoon ground turmeric

200 g (7 oz) cooked blue
swimmer crab meat

1 handful freshly grated
(or frozen) coconut (see glossary)

10 curry leaves

IDDIAPPAMS

200 g (7 oz/1 cup) iddiappam
flour (see glossary)

1 teaspoon vegetable or sunflower oil,
plus extra for greasing

To make the coconut broth, score a shallow cross in the base of the tomato. Put in a heatproof bowl and cover with boiling water. Leave for 30 seconds, then transfer to cold water and peel the skin away from the cross. Cut the tomato in half, scoop out the seeds with a teaspoon and discard. Roughly dice the flesh and set aside.

Heat the oil in a large heavy-based saucepan over medium heat, add the mustard seeds and let them crackle for 20 seconds. Add the fennel and fenugreek, onion and green chilli and cook for about 5 minutes or until the onion starts to soften. Add the turmeric, curry leaves and ginger, stir to combine, then add the tomato and coconut milk and cook for 10 minutes.

Add 160 ml (5¼ fl oz) of water, as you want a light broth that is not too thick or coconuty, and cook for 5 minutes, then season with salt. Strain the broth through a sieve and discard the solids. Set aside.

To make the iddiappams, bring 250–310 ml (9–10¾ fl oz/1–1¼ cups) of water to the boil. Add a pinch of salt and the oil. Put the flour in a large bowl and very gradually add the boiled water to make a soft dough. Knead well and form into a ball.

Grease the inside of an iddiappam mould with oil and fill with fist-sized portions of the dough at a time. When you press the mould, the dough will begin to fall out in strings. Move the mould in a circular motion, so that the strings fall onto a steaming tray to form a 7.5 cm (3 inch) diameter round — it should be a thin layer of strings, only one or two layers thick. If using a pasta maker, keep the noodles as thin as possible, finer than angel hair pasta, more like vermicelli. Repeat with the remaining dough. You should have 12 iddiappams. Steam the iddiappams for 10–15 minutes. Keep warm.

To prepare the crab topping, heat the oil in a heavy-based frying pan over medium–high heat, add the mustard seeds and let them crackle for about 20 seconds. Add the ginger, fennel, onion, green chilli and turmeric. Add the crab meat and just enough of the coconut broth to moisten the crab and toss to combine. Add the fresh coconut and curry leaves and remove from the heat.

To serve, put 2 iddiappams on each plate. Top with some crab mixture and spoon over a little of the coconut broth to moisten. Serve accompanied by a small ramekin of additional coconut broth for spooning over during eating.

duck seekh kebabs

grilled minced duck kebabs

Wanting a variation from the usual lamb and beef kebab theme, I created this recipe using duck breast meat for its light gaminess and lower fat content than other parts of the duck. It's a lightly spiced kebab as I want to highlight the flavour of the meat and not cover it up with spicing. The sweetness of the plum chutney complements the light spicing. Easy to prepare and great to eat.

400 g (14 oz) minced (ground) duck breast (ask your butcher to do this)

2 teaspoons finely grated orange zest

2 teaspoons finely chopped mint

1 tablespoon finely chopped coriander (cilantro)

½ teaspoon fennel seeds

2 teaspoons finely grated ginger

2 small red chillies, finely chopped

6 bamboo skewers, soaked in water for 20 minutes (see tip)

vegetable or sunflower oil, for brushing

fresh plum slices, to serve

plum chutney (see page 211), to serve

MAKES 6 SMALL KEBABS

Combine the duck, orange zest, herbs, fennel, ginger and chilli with a little salt in a bowl and mix well. Refrigerate for 1 hour. The mixture will be easier to work with if the meat is chilled.

Divide the mixture into six portions and mould each around a skewer.

Preheat a barbecue grill to medium. Lightly brush the grill with oil and cook the skewers for about 10 minutes, turning occasionally until golden brown and cooked through. Serve with the fresh plum slices and plum chutney.

Tip: Soaking the skewers will prevent them burning during cooking.

Feel free to experiment with how to cook the kebabs. Charcoal-fired barbecues will impart a lovely smoky flavour, which will go well with the duck meat, or you could use a chargrill pan. Whichever method you choose, take care not to overcook the meat otherwise it will be dry.

scallops tamateri

seared scallops with tomato chutney

The sweetness of the scallops marries the tomato chutney perfectly and the subtle mellow hint of the curry leaf–infused olive oil is the finishing touch. The chutney is my grandmother's recipe, except I have added onions, which she did not use in her cooking.

12–16 scallops

½ teaspoon ground turmeric

2 tablespoons vegetable oil

CURRY LEAF–INFUSED OIL

1 tablespoon gingili (unscented sesame oil) (see glossary) or sunflower oil

15 curry leaves

2 tablespoons extra virgin olive oil

TOMATO CHUTNEY

6 ripe roma (plum) tomatoes

2 tablespoons gingili (unscented sesame oil) or sunflower oil

3 dried red chillies

½ teaspoon black mustard seeds

½ teaspoon cumin seeds

1 red onion, diced

2 teaspoons Kashmiri chilli powder (see glossary)

⅛ teaspoon asafoetida (see glossary)

1 tablespoon finely grated ginger

10 curry leaves

1 teaspoon white sugar (optional)

SERVES 3–4 AS PART OF A SHARED MEAL

To make the curry leaf–infused oil, heat the gingili in a frying pan over low heat and cook the curry leaves for 30–40 seconds or until crisp. Drain on paper towel and pat dry to remove the excess oil. Crush using a mortar and pestle and mix with the olive oil. The oil will keep for up to 2 weeks.

Rub the scallops with the turmeric and set aside for 20 minutes.

Meanwhile, to make the tomato chutney, score a shallow cross in the base of the tomatoes. Put in a heatproof bowl and cover with boiling water. Leave for 30 seconds, then transfer to cold water and peel the skin away from the cross. Cut the tomatoes in half, scoop out the seeds with a teaspoon and discard. Roughly chop the flesh and set aside.

Heat the gingili in a small saucepan over medium heat, add the chillies and cook until the tips of the chillies turn black. Add the mustard seeds and let them crackle for about 20 seconds. Add the cumin and onion and cook for 5 minutes without browning. Add the chilli powder, asafoetida, ginger, curry leaves, tomato and 100 ml (3½ fl oz) of water (to soften the tomato) and cook for 15–20 minutes. If the tomato is not sweet enough, add the sugar.

To cook the scallops, heat the oil in a frying pan over high heat and sear the scallops for about 20 seconds on one side, then turn over and sear the other side for 20 seconds — do not overcook or they will become rubbery.

Serve the scallops on a bed of the chutney, drizzled with the curry leaf–infused oil.

tesri sukhé

goan clams

What a way to celebrate the fresh cashew fenny (fermented cashew liquor) at the residence of our dear friends Seema and Gautam in Goa. Seema was kind enough to share this typical home recipe with me without any hesitation.

This simple recipe does not involve any grinding of spices, major marination or much mise-en-place. In Goa, the local fishermen will open the clams with a special sickle like a knife for you. Here I have substituted baby clams in place of the Goan clams.

3 tablespoons vegetable or sunflower oil

2 teaspoons crushed garlic

2 red onions, sliced into rings

½ teaspoon ground turmeric

1 teaspoon Kashmiri chilli powder (see glossary)

1 kg (2 lb 4 oz) baby clams, soaked in water for 1 hour, then drained

2 pieces kokam (see glossary), soaked in 3 tablespoons water, or 2 teaspoons tamarind pulp

70 g (2½ oz/½ cup) grated coconut (see glossary)

½ bunch coriander (cilantro), leaves roughly chopped

green chillies, to garnish (optional)

SERVES 4–6 AS PART OF A SHARED MEAL

Heat the oil in a frying pan over medium heat. Add the garlic and lightly brown, then immediately add the onion, reserving a small handful to garnish, and cook for about 5 minutes or until soft. Add the turmeric and chilli powder and cook for 2 minutes.

Add the clams, a pinch of salt, the kokam and its soaking water, and 125 ml (4 fl oz/½ cup) of water and cook, covered, for 2–3 minutes or until the clams open.

Add the coconut and cook for 2–5 minutes, ensuring you do not brown the coconut. Add the coriander and chillies to garnish.

kumro phool bhajja

bengali pumpkin flower fritters

In Bengali cuisine, a bhaja (fritter) is an essential part of any meal. A typical Bengali plate will have some rice in the centre, surrounded by some fritters, a lentil dish and some vegetables. On one of my trips to Kolkata (Calcutta) I came across pumpkin flowers at the Lake Market (the city's fish and vegetable centre). They piqued my curiosity as they were sold alongside the vegetables and looked much like zucchini (courgette) flowers. I asked my Bengali chef friends how they were used and learned that they transform the pumpkin flower into a bhaja. Here's my take on their recipe.

12 pumpkin flowers or zucchini (courgette) flowers with baby zucchini attached

vegetable oil, for deep-frying

tamarind and ginger chutney (see page 210), to serve

FILLING

75 g (2 1/2 oz/1/4 cup) paneer (curd cheese) (see glossary), crumbled, or cottage cheese

2 teaspoons chopped coriander (cilantro) leaves

2 teaspoons sultanas (golden raisins)

1 teaspoon finely grated ginger

BATTER

90 g (3 1/4 oz/3/4 cup) chickpea flour (besan)

3 tablespoons rice flour

1/2 teaspoon finely grated ginger

1/2 teaspoon poppy seeds

1/2 teaspoon cumin seeds

1/4 teaspoon red chilli powder

1/8 teaspoon ground turmeric

SERVES 4–6 AS A STARTER OR AS PART OF A SHARED MEAL

To make the filling, crumble the paneer into a bowl, add the remaining ingredients, season with salt and combine.

Take 2 teaspoons of the filling and use to fill each pumpkin flower. Ensure you do not overstuff the flowers or they will become soggy when fried. Set aside.

To make the batter, place all of the ingredients in a bowl and stir in 185 ml (6 fl oz/3/4 cup) of water. Season with salt and gently mix to form a batter, ensuring it is not too runny.

Fill a deep-fryer or large saucepan one-third full with oil and heat to about 180°C (356°F) or until a cube of bread turns golden brown in 15 seconds. Dip the stuffed flowers, in batches, into the batter, coating them completely, and deep-fry for about 3 minutes or until golden brown, turning once to cook evenly. Remove with a slotted spoon and drain on paper towel. Serve immediately with the tamarind and ginger chutney.

sura puttu

fish hash curry

This is a common Southern Indian dish that you'll find in small restaurants all over the region. It is eaten as an accompaniment to a meal with other vegetables, lentils and rice.

2 teaspoons ground turmeric

600 g (1 lb 5 oz) hake fillets, skin removed

3 tablespoons vegetable or sunflower oil

½ teaspoon black mustard seeds

½ teaspoon fennel seeds

3 small green chillies, chopped

1½ tablespoons finely chopped ginger

8 garlic cloves, crushed

15 curry leaves

½ bunch coriander (cilantro), leaves roughly chopped

juice of 1 lime

SERVES 6 AS A SIDE DISH

Half-fill a saucepan with water, add 1 teaspoon of the turmeric and season with salt. Bring to the boil, add the fish and cook for 5 minutes. Drain the fish, then flake into pieces. Set aside.

Heat the oil in a heavy-based frying pan over medium–high heat, add the mustard seeds and let them crackle for about 20 seconds. Add the fennel seeds, chilli, ginger, garlic and remaining turmeric and cook for 1 minute, stirring regularly so the spices don't burn.

Add the fish and toss together. Add the curry leaves, coriander and lime juice. Check the seasoning and serve hot.

maan porrial

venison porrial

80 ml (2½ fl oz/⅓ cup) vegetable
or sunflower oil

800 g (1 lb 12 oz) venison
loin, diced

1 teaspoon black mustard seeds

1 teaspoon fennel seeds

2 red onions, chopped

1 tablespoon finely grated ginger

1 tablespoon sliced garlic

1 teaspoon ground fennel

2 teaspoons cracked black pepper

1 teaspoon ground turmeric

2 teaspoons red chilli powder

1 tablespoon ground coriander

1 potato, boiled and diced

45 g (1½ oz/½ cup) desiccated
coconut

juice of 1 lime

10 curry leaves

SERVES 4–6 AS PART OF A SHARED MEAL

Heat the oil in a heavy-based frying pan over high heat, add the venison, in small batches, and seal the meat all over to prevent the release of the juices during the cooking. This is a dry dish and we do not want the venison to sauce it up. Remove from the pan and set aside.

Add the mustard and fennel to the same pan over medium heat and let the mustard seeds crackle for about 20 seconds. Add the onion and cook for 6–8 minutes or until golden brown. Add the ginger and garlic and cook for about 3 minutes.

Add the venison and coat in the mixture. Add the ground fennel, pepper, turmeric, chilli powder, ground coriander, potato and coconut, gently stir to combine and cook for 5 minutes or until the venison is cooked.

Stir in the lime juice, scatter over the curry leaves and serve.

punjabi bheh masala

lotus root curry

A very dear family friend from Delhi served us this wonderful dish and shared this recipe with us. That was my first time eating lotus root and I was extremely fascinated with the texture of the vegetable. This is a very North Indian dish popular in Kashmir and Punjab. The Kashmiris cook this in yoghurt and ghee, while I have made this preparation in mustard oil and poppy seeds.

500 g (1 lb 2 oz) lotus root

2 tablespoons poppy seeds

1 teaspoon ground turmeric

3 tablespoons mustard oil (see glossary)

2 teaspoons cumin seeds

3 red onions, grated

1 tablespoon finely grated ginger

1 teaspoon red chilli powder

1 tablespoon ground coriander

3 small green chillies, roughly chopped

red chilli powder and finely chopped coriander (cilantro), to garnish (optional)

SERVES 4 AS PART OF A SHARED MEAL

Cut the lotus root into thin slices on an angle and soak in cold water for 1 hour.

Soak the poppy seeds in 3 tablespoons of water for 20 minutes (see tip). Put the poppy seeds and soaking water in a spice grinder or small blender and grind to a fine paste.

Drain the lotus root. Bring a saucepan of water to the boil with ½ teaspoon of the turmeric, add the lotus root and cook for 20–30 minutes or until soft. Drain and set aside.

Heat 1 tablespoon of the mustard oil in a heavy-based frying pan over medium–high heat, add the cumin and let them crackle for about 20 seconds. Add the onion and cook until brown. Add the poppy seed paste and cook, stirring constantly, for about 3 minutes, adding a little extra oil to prevent the poppy seed paste from sticking to the pan.

Once the onion and poppy seeds turn a darker brown, stir in 1 tablespoon of water. Add the ginger, remaining turmeric, chilli powder and ground coriander and cook over low heat for 5 minutes, stirring regularly.

Add the lotus root and green chilli. Keep stirring until the sauce has thickened and coats the lotus root. Season with salt.

Tip: Soaking the poppy seeds makes it easier to grind them.

mishti dohi

baked sweet yoghurt cream

I discovered this dish on my recent travels to Kolkata (Calcutta). Traditionally, these are baked in clay pots, which aids setting, but then the pot is broken when you've finished (for hygiene, so it's not re-used). We were served this for breakfast and I was enamoured. What an excellent way to start the day or finish a meal.

100 ml (3½ fl oz) thick (double/heavy) cream

130 g (4½ oz) sweetened condensed milk

100 g (3½ oz) plain thick yoghurt

½ teaspoon ground cardamom

1 tablespoon coarsely ground pistachio nuts (optional)

3 tablespoons pomegranate seeds (optional)

SERVES 4 FOR BREAKFAST OR AS A DESSERT

Preheat the oven to 180°C (350°F/Gas 4).

Put the cream, milk, yoghurt and cardamom in a bowl and mix thoroughly, then strain through a sieve into a bowl.

Divide the mixture among four 80 ml (2½ fl oz/⅓ cup) capacity ramekins and put in a baking dish. Pour hot water into the dish to come about halfway up the sides of the ramekins.

Bake for 15–20 minutes or until firmly set, keeping an eye on them. Remove from the water bath and leave to cool to room temperature.

Serve in the ramekins at room temperature or chilled, garnished with the pistachio nuts and pomegranate seeds.

ledikeni

bengali semolina doughnuts

On our recent visit to Kolkata (Calcutta), we came across this dessert that resembles gulab jamun (fried doughnuts soaked in syrup) but is slightly different. Ledikeni is the traditional Bengali dessert called pantua but it was renamed in honour of Lady Canning, wife of Governor-General Charles Canning, who visited the local sweet shops of Calcutta in 1856.

500 g (1 lb 2 oz) white sugar

3 teaspoons rosewater

**350 g (12 oz) paneer (curd cheese)
(see glossary) (see tip)**

2 tablespoons fine semolina

**150 g (5½ oz/1⅓ cups)
milk powder**

3 tablespoons self-raising flour

**3 black cardamom pods,
seeds only (see tip)**

**500 g (1 lb 2 oz) ghee
(see glossary), melted**

**100 g (3½ oz) caster (superfine)
sugar**

18 raisins

SERVES 6 AS A DESSERT

Put the white sugar, rosewater and 250 ml (9 fl oz/1 cup) of water in a saucepan over medium heat and slowly bring to the boil, stirring to dissolve the sugar. Continue to boil for 3 minutes. Set aside to cool slightly (see tip).

Put the paneer, semolina, milk powder, flour, cardamom seeds, 1 tablespoon of the ghee and 2 tablespoons of the caster sugar in a large bowl and knead to a doughy consistency. Set aside for 15 minutes.

Portion the dough into 18 balls. Push a raisin into the centre of each ball and roll into a cylindrical shape.

Heat the remaining ghee in a wok or heavy-based saucepan to 160°C (320°F) or until a cube of bread browns in 30–35 seconds. Fry the dough balls for about 3 minutes, turning occasionally until slightly darker than golden brown. Remove with a slotted spoon and drain on paper towel. Immerse the cooked dough in the prepared sugar syrup and leave to soak for 2 hours.

To serve, sprinkle the remaining caster sugar onto a large sheet of baking paper. Remove the balls from the syrup, allowing the excess to drip off, and roll in the sugar.

Tip: You can substitute the paneer with fresh ricotta cheese.
Green cardamoms can be substituted for the black version.
The temperature of the sugar syrup should be slightly on the warmer side, so when the doughnuts are added to it, the syrup will be able to seep through and flavour them.

pineapple kesari

pineapple semolina cake

This is a dessert that is very close to my heart. It has been a favourite of mine since childhood, but it became more special when my prospective mother-in-law served it to me when I met Suba for the first time. It is a popular sweet in South India and is one of those dishes that can be quickly conjured up if an unannounced visitor lands on your doorstep.

125 g (4½ oz/½ cup) ghee (see glossary), melted

15 g (½ oz) cashew nuts, chopped into small pieces

150 g (5½ oz) coarse semolina (see tip)

300 g (10½ oz) caster (superfine) sugar

10 saffron threads

50 g (1¾ oz) pineapple, finely diced

3 green cardamom pods, crushed

2 tablespoons sultanas (golden raisins)

Place 1 tablespoon of the ghee in a small frying pan over medium heat and fry the cashews until golden brown. Set aside.

Heat a large dry heavy-based saucepan over low heat, add the semolina and lightly toast for 1 minute to remove the moisture. Add 400 ml (14 fl oz) of water and cook for about 5–7 minutes, stirring constantly. Once the semolina has softened, add the sugar, saffron, pineapple and cardamom pods — this will turn the mixture a little watery. Gently cook for 4–5 minutes or until the sugar has dissolved, stirring constantly so the sugar does not caramelise on the bottom.

Slowly pour the remaining ghee into the semolina and cook for 5 minutes. By this point, the mixture should leave the sides of the pan and not stick to the base. It should appear a bit oily (see tip).

Stir half of the fried cashews and all of the sultanas into the semolina and serve warm with the remaining cashews sprinkled over the top. This is a very sweet dish, so you only need a small portion per person.

Tip: Coarse semolina is preferred rather than the fine variety.

The kesari should not be sticky to the fingers. There is a generous amount of ghee used so it does not stick to the eating utensils and also for its great taste.

You can replace the pineapple with other flavours such as apricot and candied ginger.

condiments
& sides

green chutney

coriander & chilli chutney

½ bunch mint, leaves picked

1 bunch coriander (cilantro), leaves picked and coarsely chopped

4 long green chillies, chopped

½ red onion

1 tablespoon lemon juice

2 teaspoons finely grated ginger

MAKES ABOUT 1½ CUPS

Process all of the ingredients with 1 teaspoon of salt and ½ teaspoon of ground black pepper in a food processor until smooth. Transfer to a small bowl and cover until ready to serve.

tamarind & ginger chutney

3 tablespoons gingili (unscented sesame oil) (see glossary)

6 dried red chillies

1 teaspoon black mustard seeds

2 tablespoons finely grated ginger

80 ml (2½ fl oz/⅓ cup) tamarind concentrate (see glossary)

150 g (5½ oz/1 cup) grated palm sugar (jaggery)

MAKES ABOUT 1½ CUPS

Heat the gingili in a small saucepan over medium–high heat, add the chillies and cook until blackened. Add the mustard seeds and allow them to crackle for 20 seconds.

Add the ginger, tamarind concentrate and 200 ml (7 fl oz) of water and bring to the boil. Add the palm sugar and cook for 20 minutes or until it is thick enough to coat a spoon. Remove from the heat and set aside to cool. Store in an airtight jar in the fridge for up to 2 weeks.

plum chutney

500 g (1 lb 2 oz) red plums, stones removed and finely diced

100 ml (3½ fl oz) white vinegar

100 g (3½ oz) white sugar

1 cinnamon stick

2–3 green cardamom pods

2–3 black peppercorns

3–4 g (⅛ oz) Kashmiri chilli powder (see glossary)

1 g (¹⁄₃₂ oz) finely chopped garlic

MAKES 600–700 ML (21–24 FL OZ)

Combine all of the ingredients in a saucepan over low heat and cook for 15–20 minutes or until thickened, stirring occassionally. Remove from the heat, then transfer to the fridge to chill. Serve cold. Store in an airtight container in the fridge for up to 1 week.

burrani raita

520 g (1 lb 2½ oz/2 cups) plain thick yoghurt

12 garlic cloves

½ teaspoon red chilli powder

3 tablespoons milk

ground cumin, to garnish

MAKES ABOUT 2 CUPS

Beat the yoghurt until smooth and set aside.

Crush the garlic, then pass through a fine sieve to collect the juice. Discard the solids.

Add the garlic juice and chilli powder to the yoghurt, season with salt and mix well. Add enough milk to achieve a thin consistency. Chill until ready to serve.

Garnish with a pinch of cumin and serve with biriyani.

chettiyar chutney

6 onions, roughly chopped

10 roma (plum) tomatoes, peeled and roughly chopped

8–10 dried red chillies

275 g (9¾ oz) tamarind concentrate (see glossary)

75 g (2½ oz) chana dal (see glossary), toasted

8 thin garlic slices

1 tablespoon gingili (unscented sesame oil) (see glossary)

1 teaspoon black mustard seeds

MAKES ABOUT 1½ CUPS

Place all of the ingredients, except the gingili and mustard seeds, in a food processor and process until finely chopped and smooth. Transfer to a bowl.

Heat the oil in a frying pan over medium–high heat, add the mustard seeds and allow them to crackle for 20 seconds. Remove from the heat and add to the onion mixture.

mint & yoghurt sauce

1 bunch mint, leaves and stalks

1 bunch coriander (cilantro), leaves and stalks

2 small green chillies

2 garlic cloves

1 tablespoon finely grated ginger

1 teaspoon cumin seeds

1 teaspoon white sugar

10 black peppercorns

500 g (1 lb 2 oz) plain thick yoghurt

juice of 1 lime

MAKES ABOUT 1½ CUPS

Roughly chop the herb leaves and stalks and place in a food processor. Add the remaining ingredients, except the lime juice and yoghurt, and process to a smooth paste, adding minimal water as necessary.

Place the yoghurt in a bowl and beat until smooth. Add the herb mixture and lime juice, and season with salt. Refrigerate until needed.

(pictured page 216)

tamarind rice

500 g (1 lb 2 oz/2½ cups) long-grain white rice, rinsed

180 ml (5¾ fl oz) vegetable or sunflower oil

1 teaspoon black mustard seeds

5 dried red chillies

½ teaspoon fenugreek seeds

pinch of asafoetida (see glossary)

1 teaspoon ground turmeric

125 ml (4 fl oz/½ cup) tamarind water (see glossary)

1 tablespoon chana dal (see glossary)

1 tablespoon raw peanuts

1 tablespoon coriander seeds, toasted and ground

1 tablespoon sesame seeds, toasted and ground

10 fried curry leaves

SERVES 4

Place the rice in a saucepan, cover with 2.5 cm (1 inch) of water and bring to the boil over medium heat. Once it is three-quarters cooked, drain the rice, spread it over a tray and allow it to dry completely and cool to room temperature.

Drizzle 80 ml (2½ fl oz/⅓ cup) of the oil over the rice.

Heat 80 ml (2½ fl oz/⅓ cup) of the oil in a small saucepan over medium–high heat, add the mustard seeds and let them crackle for 20 seconds, then add the chillies, fenugreek, asafoetida and turmeric. Add the tamarind water, season with salt and cook for 3 minutes or until thick like a gravy.

Heat the remaining oil in a small frying pan over medium heat, add the chana dal and peanuts and cook until golden brown. Add to the rice.

Add the ground coriander seeds and sesame seeds, tamarind mixture and curry leaves to the rice, mix well and serve.

lemon rice

500 g (1 lb 2 oz/2½ cups) long-grain white rice, rinsed

1 tablespoon vegetable or sunflower oil

1 teaspoon black mustard seeds

pinch of asafoetida (see glossary)

1 teaspoon chana dal (see glossary)

1 teaspoon urad dal (black lentils/black gram) (see glossary)

2 dried red chillies, broken in half

2 small green chillies, chopped

½ teaspoon ground turmeric

juice of 3 lemons

1 tablespoon fried cashew nuts

1 tablespoon fried peanuts

10 fried curry leaves

Place the rice in a saucepan, cover with 2.5 cm (1 inch) of water and bring to the boil over medium heat. Cook until al dente. Drain the water and place the rice in a large bowl.

Heat the oil in a small frying pan over medium–high heat, add the mustard seeds and allow them to crackle for 20 seconds, then add the asafoetida, chana dal, urad dal, and dried and green chillies and cook until the dal is golden brown. Add the turmeric, then remove from the heat and set aside to cool to room temperature.

Add the lemon juice to the spice mixture, then pour the mixture over the rice, season with salt and mix well. Garnish with the fried nuts and curry leaves.

Tip Make sure mixture has cooled to room temperature before adding the lemon juice otherwise it will taste bitter.

curd rice

500 g (1 lb 2 oz/2½ cups) long-grain white rice, rinsed

1 tablespoon vegetable oil

½ teaspoon black mustard seeds

1 dried red chilli, broken in half

125 ml (4 fl oz/½ cup) milk

3 small green chillies, chopped

3 cm (1¼ inch) piece of ginger, chopped

10 curry leaves

1.3 kg (3 lb/5 cups) fresh curd or plain thick yoghurt

SERVES 4

Place the rice in a saucepan, cover with 2.5 cm (1 inch) of water and bring to the boil over medium heat. Cook until al dente. Drain the water, place the rice in a large bowl and allow to cool.

Heat the oil in a frying pan over medium–high heat, add the mustard seeds and allow them to crackle for 20 seconds, then add the dried and green chillies, ginger and curry leaves and cook until fragrant but not coloured. Remove from the heat and add to the rice.

Add the curd, season with salt and stir, then add the milk and mix thoroughly. This is best eaten with lime pickle.

coconut rice

500 g (1 lb 2 oz/2½ cups) long-grain white rice, rinsed

2 tablespoons coconut oil

½ teaspoon black mustard seeds

pinch of asafoetida (see glossary)

1 tablespoon chana dal (see glossary)

1 teaspoon urad dal (black lentils/black gram) (see glossary)

2 dried red chillies, broken in half

1 small green chilli, halved lengthways

1 coconut, flesh grated

10 curry leaves

1 tablespoon fried cashew nuts

SERVES 4

Place the rice in a saucepan, cover with 2.5 cm (1 inch) of water and bring to the boil over medium heat. Cook until al dente. Drain the water and place the rice in a large bowl.

Heat the oil in a frying pan over medium–high heat, add the mustard seeds and allow them to crackle for 20 seconds, then add the asafoetida, chana dal, urad dal, and dried and green chillies and cook until the dal turns golden brown.

Add the coconut and cook until fragrant but not coloured. Remove from the heat, stir in the curry leaves and season with salt.

Pour the spice mixture over the rice and mix well. Garnish with the fried cashew nuts.

rasam powder

8 dried red chillies

2 tablespoons coriander seeds

20 black peppercorns

1 tablespoon cumin seeds

2 tablespoons toor dal (yellow lentils) (see glossary)

1 tablespoon chana dal (see glossary)

1 teaspoon ground turmeric

MAKES ABOUT ½ CUP

In a dry frying pan over medium heat, lightly toast all the ingredients, shaking the pan occasionally so they don't burn. Using a spice grinder or mortar and pestle, grind into a fine powder. Store in an airtight jar for up to 6 months.

chapatis

500 g (1 lb 2 oz/3⅓ cups) plain (all-purpose) flour or wholemeal atta flour (see glossary)

1 teaspoon salt

1 tablespoon ghee (see glossary) or butter, for greasing

Sift the flour into a large bowl and make a well in the centre. While mixing with your hand, gradually add 300 ml (10½ fl oz) of water, kneading until a smooth dough forms. Add the salt and knead to combine. Cover with a lid or plastic wrap and set aside for 20–30 minutes.

Lightly knead the dough again, then divide it into 18–20 rounded portions.

With your palms lightly greased with a little ghee, flatten each portion and lightly dust with flour so it doesn't stick to the work surface, then roll it into a thin 13 cm (5 inch) diameter round using a rolling pin.

Heat a dry frying pan or tava over medium–high heat and when hot, place the chapati in the pan and cook until small air pockets start to bubble up, then turn over and lightly cook the other side.

Once it is cooked on both sides, gently press the sides down using a clean cloth. This will make the chapati swell. Once puffed, remove from the fire and serve hot.

Repeat with the remaining dough.

Tip: You can make the chapatis about 20 minutes ahead of time. Keep them wrapped in a tea towel and store in an airtight container — this will ensure they remain soft. You can also smear some ghee over the top before serving.

(pictured page 216)

puri

225 g (8 oz/1½ cups) plain (all-purpose) flour or wholemeal atta flour (see glossary)

1 teaspoon salt

80 g (2¾ oz) ghee (see glossary), for greasing

vegetable or sunflower oil, for deep-frying

MAKES ABOUT 10

Sift the flour into a large bowl and make a well in the centre. While mixing with your hand, gradually add 100 ml (3½ fl oz) of water, kneading until a thick dough forms. Add the salt and knead to combine. Cover with a lid or plastic wrap and set aside for 30 minutes.

Lightly knead the dough again, then divide it into golf-ball-sized portions.

With your palms lightly greased with a little ghee, flatten each portion and lightly dust with flour so it doesn't stick to the work surface, then roll it into a thin 7.5–10 cm (3–4 inch) diameter round using a rolling pin. Repeat with the remaining dough balls.

Heat the oil in a small deep-sided saucepan to 180°C (356°F) or until a cube of bread turns golden brown in 15 seconds and deep-fry the puri, one at a time. Using a large slotted spoon, keep the puri under the oil. This helps the puri to puff up. Once it is puffed and golden brown, remove from the oil with the slotted spoon and serve immediately. Repeat with the remaining puri.

(pictured page 217)

glossary

amchur *(dry mango powder)* A souring agent widely used in North India. It is derived from powdered sun-dried green mangoes. Used primarily to sprinkle on chaat and tandoori preparations.

asafoetida *(hing)* A highly aromatic spice derived from the root of the ferula asafoetida plant. It is primarily imported from Iran. Although very pungent in its raw form, adding it to hot oil gives a rich onion-like flavour to dishes. In Hindu cooking, garlic and asafoetida are not used together as they provide similar flavours. Asafoetida is also used for its medicinal properties as it aids digestion. It is generally used in its powdered form and is available from Indian grocery stores in little containers.

atta flour A high-gluten flour used to make unleavened Indian breads such as chapati, puri, naan and paratha. It's available at Indian grocery stores.

black chickpeas *(kala chana)* Also known as bengal gram, these are a variety of lentil. Unlike regular chickpeas, these are dark brown in colour, smaller in size and harder. They need to be soaked overnight before cooking. Chana dal is made from kala chana by removing the skins and splitting them in half.

black cumin seeds *(jeera)* Cumin comes from the same family as fennel, caraway and aniseed. It is used whole and in powdered form. It's a delicate spice and will turn bitter if cooked for more than a minute. It is used to temper dry vegetarian dishes and pullaos.

cardamom, *black & green* Green cardamom is sourced mainly from South India and Sri Lanka. It is used whole and in powdered form. It is also one of the main ingredients in a garam masala. Crushed cardamom seeds are also used in sweet dishes. Black cardamom is grown in the Himalayan foothills. It is bigger than its green counterpart and has an earthy/woody flavour. It is used in garam masalas, too, and also in pullaos in North Indian cooking.

carom seeds *(ajwain)* Ajwain comes from the same family of plants as coriander, cumin and fennel. It is also known as bishop's weed, caraway seeds or thymol seeds. It is usually used in its seed form, as a flavouring agent in batters and as a part of tempering (tadka). It has a strong flavour and is therefore used in small quantities. It aids digestion and helps to control nausea.

cassia bark Also referred to as Chinese cinnamon, it is an aromatic bark closely related to cinnamon. It is harder than cinnamon and has a darker woody look. It's used in either powdered form or whole, and forms part of garam masalas.

chana dal This is a derivative of the black chickpea where the skin has been removed and the kernel has been split in half. It looks like yellow split peas but is different as it does not readily boil down and collapse like the yellow split peas. It is available at Indian grocery stores.

charoli *(chironji)* Known as chironji in Hindi, it is the soft seed centre of a bush cultivated in northwest India. It is primarily used in sweets and as a thickening agent for gravies. It has a sweetish flavour.

chilli powder, *kashmiri, red & yellow*
Chilli is an integral part of all Indian cuisines.
There are a variety of chillies and chilli powders,
based on regions, and their use is dictated by their
characteristics. The Kashmiri chilli is a dark-
coloured and mild-flavoured chilli. It imparts a deep
red colour when used in dishes and is medium hot.
It is similar to paprika but it has more heat. The red
chilli is the most commonly used chilli powder. It
provides a strong, biting heat. Always add it in small
quantities. You can always add a little more later.
The yellow chilli is primarily used in Northern/
Mughlai cuisine. It is used for its yellow colour to
give a rich golden look to dishes and strong heat.

coconut Coconut is a widely used ingredient
in Southern Indian cooking. It is used in a multitude
of forms such as: desiccated, oil, milk, cream and
paste. It has a sweet flavour and is a good binding
agent for some dishes. Freshly grated coconut is
the white pulp of a coconut. It is available at Indian
grocery stores frozen in packets. Most other forms
are readily available in supermarkets.

curry leaves Curry leaves are an important
aromatic ingredient in Southern Indian dishes.
They can be used fresh or dried, though the fresh
leaves are more flavourful. They do not keep well
under refrigeration and have a short shelf life. They
are usually added to hot oil to release their flavour.
They are used for garnishes and tempering.

dried fenugreek leaves Known as
kasuri methi in Hindi, these are the dried leaves of
the fenugreek plant. They have a bitter taste and are
used in small quantities. They are readily available
at Indian grocery stores.

dried kashmiri red chillies *see chilli
powder, kashimiri, red & yellow*

drumstick The muringa kai (in Tamil) is the
long, slender green seed pod of the drumstick tree.
It is used widely in Southern Indian dishes. It is
very fibrous and has a hard outer skin. It needs to be
chopped into segments about 5–8 cm (2–3¼ inches)
because the inside of the pod is what we need to
cook. The outer shell is not eaten but is chewed upon
to get to the soft seed and flesh inside. It must be
well cooked in sauces. It is readily available at Indian
grocery stores fresh, cut, frozen and tinned.

garam masala The word garam, meaning
hot, relates to the intensity of spice, and masala
means a combination of different spices. So garam
masala refers to any blend of spices, and can be
either whole or powdered. All Indian households
would use a garam masala but the ingredients
differ according to recipe requirements and
personal choice. A typical Indian garam masala
contains: black peppercorns, cloves, cinnamon,
cumin and cardamom.

ghee This is clarified butter, readily available in
Indian stores. Ghee features prominently in Punjabi
cuisine where it is used to give richness to food.
Most Indian sweets are made with ghee. It has a long
shelf life and does not need refrigeration.

gingili *(unscented sesame oil)* This is a vegetable
oil derived from sesame seeds. Unlike sesame seed
oil used in southeastern cuisines, this one has no
scent. It is called nalla ennai (in Tamil) meaning,
good oil.

iddiappam flour Iddiappam is a traditional culinary speciality of South India consisting of rice flour pressed into noodle form, shaped into round cakes and then steamed. Hand-pounded rice flour is used to make iddiappam. Both white and brown rice flour are used. These are available in South Indian or Sri Lankan grocery stores.

kewra water *(pandanus water)* This is an extract distilled from pandanus flowers. It is a clear liquid, similar to rosewater, and can be used in meat dishes, rice biriyanis and sweets. It is a strong flavouring so care must be taken when adding it to preparations. It stores well, for up to a year at room temperature and longer if refrigerated. Care must be taken that the cap is sealed well as the strong scent can be hard to get rid of from other things.

kithul jaggery This is the natural palm sugar of Sri Lanka. It's a dark brown jaggery. It is used as a natural alternative to processed sugar as it is all natural, and preservative and chemical free. It is made from the sap of the young kithul palm. Available in Sri Lankan grocery stores.

kokam A member of the mangosteen family, the kokam bears a purple coloured fruit that is used as a souring agent in western coastal cooking. The outer cover of the fruit is sun dried and that is used in cooking. It gives a sour taste and a darkish purple colour to the dish. The flavour profile is similar to tamarind, which is used more in South India.

moong dal *(green gram)* These are whole green mung beans. These need to be soaked in water before they can be cooked into a dal. This bean is also skinned and split in half to reveal a pale yellow colour and it is used for making pancake batter and yellow-hued dals.

mustard oil It is a fatty vegetable oil used predominantly in Northern Indian cooking. It has a strong pungent odour and is therefore heated almost to smoking point before cooking in order to reduce the smell and taste. It can be produced from both black mustard and white mustard seeds. It is considered to assist hair regeneration, and improve skin texture and vision.

nigella seeds *(onion seeds/kalonji)* These are small black seeds used in Indian cooking as a mild substitute for pepper. These seeds have very little smell but release their flavour when heated. Nigella seeds are also one of the five ingredients in panch phoran masala (see below). These are not related to onions at all, but the name seems to have stuck from a perception of its onion-like smell.

palm vinegar This is a white cloudy vinegar made from the fermented sap of the palm flower. It can be used as a substitute for toddy vinegar.

panch phoran masala Literally translated to five spices, it is a mix of whole spices used in Eastern Indian cooking. The five spices are: fennel, mustard, nigella, fenugreek and cumin seeds in equal proportions. Fenugreek seeds may be reduced to avoid a bitter taste. Panch phoran masala is usually used whole, not powdered.

paneer This is a fresh cottage cheese made from curdling heated milk by adding lemon juice or vinegar. The curdled milk is then hung in muslin (cheesecloth) and the excess water content (that is, the whey) is drained out of the cheese. The curds can then be pressed into blocks or left in their scrambled form as well. It's available in the refrigerated section of Indian grocery stores.

paratha This is a generic term for an Indian flatbread made from wholemeal atta or plain flour. There are many types of parathas with different textures or fillings.

roti A staple unleavened Indian bread made from wholemeal atta, usually cooked on a hotplate or griddle.

tamarind, *pulp, concentrate & water*
Tamarind is the pod-like fruit of the tamarind tree. The pulp of the ripened brown pod is extracted for cooking. It is used extensively across India to add a sour and piquant taste to dishes. The pulp is available in Indian stores as a block. This needs to be loosened in hot water to make a thick mixture that is then strained and the resulting 'tamarind water' is used in cooking. Indian grocery stores also sell tamarind concentrate, which is basically a ready-made, more concentrated version of the pulp prepared as above.

tempering This is the process by which spices are added to heated oil in order to release their individual flavours. It can be done either at the beginning of a dish or added onto a cooked preparation at the end.

toddy vinegar The toddy vinegar of Goa dates back to the influx of the Portuguese settlers, who introduced fermented palm wine, called toddy. The Christians in Goa use this toddy to make vinegar, which is used in meat and fish dishes as a souring agent. It should be added in the final stages of cooking as it will turn bitter if cooked for long. It is not readily available outside of Goa so it may be substituted with either palm or malt vinegar.

toor dal *(yellow lentils)* These are yellow split peas and are used in the preparation of the popular South Indian dish sambar. These are high-protein pulses, which are used heavily across India, predominantly in a vegetarian diet. These cook easily and do not require extended soaking.

urad dal *(black lentils, black gram)* Whole urad dal is a black-skinned pulse that is used to make the popular dal makhni. The whole urad needs to be soaked overnight and then slow-cooked extensively to achieve a rich creamy flavour. In South India, the urad dal is dehulled and split to be used in batters for dosas and idlis. It is also used in the tempering of dishes as it gives a nutty and crunchy texture.

white poppy seeds Also known as khus-khus, these are used primarily as a thickening agent in Mughlai dishes. The seeds are soaked in water and then ground to a smooth paste.

acknowledgements

A big thanks, *nanri* as we say in Tamil, to Murdoch Books, which has helped us in our journey of creating our first cookbook. Our heartiest thanks to Sally Webb and the Murdoch Books team, who took this book as their own, from the beginning to the end. Our thanks to Laura Wilson (Project Editor), Tania Gomes (Designer), Michelle Noerianto (Stylist), Mark Roper (Photographer), Livia Caiazzo (Managing Editor), Belinda So (Editor), Katy Holder (Food Editor), Brett Sargent, Olivia Andrews and Grace Campbell. Without you guys, the outcome would not have been as beautiful as it is.

To Les Luxford for his support and advice through the years, and also for being kind enough to write the foreword for this book.

To Simon Thompson for editing our story and giving it the voice for our feelings.

To Mohanchandran (Taj General Manager) and Seema, you shall always be remembered for the help you extended to us on our travels to India towards discovering the depth of Indian cuisine.

Thank you to Chef Praveen Anand (Park Sheraton, Chennai), who we could always refer to as our encyclopaedia on Southern Indian Cuisine for research. We would like to thank all the chefs from India who assisted us in the recipe research: Chef Amit Choudhury (Taj Palace, Delhi), Chef Sujaon Mukherjee (Taj Bengal), Chef Ganesh Joshi (Taj Srinagar), Chef Narendra Singh (Taj Lucknow), and Chef Valentine (Taj Lucknow).

Thanks to Luke Nguyen and Susanna for getting us started on this wonderful project.

Thanks to the teams at Abhi's and Aki's — Chefs Ranjan and Vikram, for their ever-present support. Special thanks to Akshay for all the tireless, late night 'recipe cooking' with the right spirit.

index

Published in 2013 by Murdoch Books Pty Limited

Murdoch Books Australia
83 Alexander Street
CROWS NEST
NSW 2065
Phone: +61 (0) 2 8425 0100
Fax: +61 (0) 2 9906 2218
www.murdochbooks.com.au
info@murdochbooks.com.au

Murdoch Books UK Limited
Erico House, 6th Floor
93–99 Upper Richmond Road
Putney, London SW15 2TG
Phone: +44 (0) 20 8785 5995
Fax: +44 (0) 20 8785 5985
www.murdochbooks.co.uk
info@murdochbooks.co.uk

For Corporate Orders & Custom Publishing contact Noel Hammond,
National Business Development Manager Murdoch Books Australia

Publisher: Sally Webb
Designer: Tania Gomes
Photographer: Mark Roper
Stylist: Michelle Noerianto
Editor: Belinda So
Food Editor: Katy Holder
Project Managers: Laura Wilson, Livia Caiazzo
Production Manager: Karen Small
Additional text by Simon Thomsen

A cataloguing-in-publication entry is available from the catalogue of the National
Library of Australia at www.nla.gov.au.

A catalogue record for this book is available from the British Library.

Printed by 1010 Printing International Limited, China.

The Publisher and stylist would like to thank Ruby Star Traders for lending their
unique Indian homewares and textiles for photography.

IMPORTANT: Those who might be at risk from the effects of salmonella
poisoning (the elderly, pregnant women, young children and those suffering
from immune deficiency diseases) should consult their doctor with any concerns
about eating raw eggs.

OVEN GUIDE: You may find cooking times vary depending on the oven you are
using. For fan-forced ovens, as a general rule, set the oven temperature to 20°C
(35°F) lower than indicated in the recipe.

We have used 20 ml (4 teaspoon) tablespoon measures. If you are using a 15
ml (3 teaspoon) tablespoon add an extra teaspoon of the ingredient for each
tablespoon specified.